Ocean WhiteHawk is an educator,
metaphysicist, writer, motivational speaker
and self-empowerment coach.

She also teaches 'A Course in Miracles'
and specialises in the fields of spirituality
and metaphysics. Her passion is to help
every woman awaken her inner bliss.

www.oceanwhitehawk.com

Juicy Woman™

A Spiritual Guide To Your Feminine Radiance

Ocean WhiteHawk

Published by JuicySpirituality.Com
United Kingdom

Published by
JuicySpirituality.Com
The Corner House
Station Road
Thorpe-le-Soken
Essex CO16 0HD
United Kingdom
www.juicyspirituality.com

Greenpeace approved FSC certified paper carry FSC logo.

One sterling pound from the sale of each book goes to 'ConfidentWoman',
a charitable organisation founded by the author in England. It offers free courses
and coaching to help and support women with limited financial means to develop
a healthy self-esteem and vibrant confidence in their personal and working life.

Printed and bound in Great Britain by Lavenham Press, Suffolk
A CIP catalogue record for this book is available from the British Library
ISBN 978-0-9562538-0-4

To every woman.
May you return to Love.
May you behold the glory of your divine femininity,
and bless the world with your radiance.

CONTENTS

Your Juicy Essence

Your Juicy Beauty

Your Juicy Relationship with Man

Juicy Sisterhood

Reading Map

The scope of the material in this book is immense. It contains spiritual insights that will help you remember what is real and good inside you. It is a compass that points you to your own heart so that you can unearth the wisdom you've been seeking. It translates the spiritual principles that govern life into an everyday language, for you to work in harmony with everything around you. It recontextualises the way you look at reality so that you can receive the gift that is offered in every moment.

The style of presentation is precise, in a language that allows your heart to feel the truth and claim this truth which is already within you with your conscious mind. A wisdom page precedes every chapter, its purpose is to open your mind and spark your higher awareness to see truth in a new light. The prose in the wisdom pages are the author's own. Each chapter concludes with a paragraph in italics, to remind you of what the JuicyWoman in you would do in each blessed scenario.

At the first glance, some of the material in the book may seem repetitious. This is deliberate because each time it is presented in a different context it allows your subconscious mind to absorb the teachings deeper.

The word 'love' is sometimes written with a capital 'L' and at other times not. This is to differentiate the polarity between the two. When it is written as 'Love' it represents the unchanging and immovable divine nature which is innate in all sentient beings. When written in lower case, it simply denotes a transient emotion of human nature.

To get the best out of the book, you only have to be willing to open your mind and let go of the old ideas in your head. Your own wisdom will flood in to illuminate your being. With regular practise and diligent effort towards your spiritual development, you will be lifted to the glorious summit of your own radiant self.

My Journey

My childhood was one of pain and fear, of sadness, lack of love and, ultimately, betrayed trust. I could have been badly damaged by my experiences, instead I managed to turn them into a beautiful gift, which I want to share with you. But first I must open my heart and tell you my story.

My parents separated when I was one. My mother was only allowed to have custody over one of us and she had to choose between my sister, who was three, and me. The two elder boys were out of bounds as they were my paternal grandmother's favourites. She had come from China to settle in Malaysia with my grandfather, and she still held the typical Chinese view that boys are more precious and valuable than girls. Initially, my mother wanted to keep my sister with her, but my sister would not go, and so she took me.

At that time in Malaysia there was no help given to single mothers. If you didn't work, you didn't eat. So, for ten years, I was left with my mother's friends while she earned the money to feed and clothe us both. For the first couple of years, my father visited us from time to time, but those visits stopped when my parents' relationship became too strained. I was still very young, and for a long time I had no recollection of my father. I used to wonder why I didn't have a father in my life. I was bold enough to ask my mother once and she curtly told me that I had been born from a stone. With a scar across my cheek and a birth defect on my ear, I already felt different to the other children, so her remark didn't seem so strange. At five, I had no concept about 'the birds and the bees', so I thought perhaps I had come out of a stone.

When my mother went further afield to work, months would go by before I would see her. Those visits were brief, and whenever it was time for her to leave I would cry my heart out. I felt desperate, not because I missed my mother's affection, as she only had cold stares for me, but because, on my own, I was vulnerable to the cruel taunts and antics of the other children who were part of the community we lived in. I was 'Scar Face' to them, and I would have to do their chores, like sweeping the courtyard and doing the washing-up, before they would include me in their games.

There were some brief periods of happiness during this phase of lodging with my mother's friends. These moments of joy came when I was roaming freely in nature, watching butterflies dance amongst the flowers, and I would disappear into a mental fantasy of a perfect life where I didn't endure beatings from my frustrated mother whenever she visited me. If she saw me every six months, there would be six months worth of tales of how naughty I had been. This would infuriate her greatly. Once, she lost control and caned me incessantly, crying and lashing out violently at the same time. It went on for so long that a neighbour had to climb over the wooden partitioned wall to rescue me. At the time, I thought the beating was never going to stop.

At the age of eight, I couldn't make much sense of it all, except that I felt guilty for causing my mother so much heartache and unhappiness. It was during such times that she ranted about my father not wanting me (that was when I realised that my father existed), and how she had never wanted me either. If she had not had me, she used to say, she would have had a better life. I already felt abandoned, so being blamed like this made the pain even more acute. I concluded that there must be something wrong with me, that somehow I was not good enough to deserve the acceptance, never mind the love, of my parents.

When I was ten, my mother remarried and decided that I should live with her and her new husband in the city. On the journey to my new home, as we were nearing our destination, my mother turned to me and said from that point on I had to call her 'Aunty'. With that she turned away and continued to gaze out of the window of the cab we were in. I didn't understand why she wanted me to call her Aunty until I overheard her telling a neighbour that I was her sister's child. That didn't bother me, as I was elated that I could live with my mother at last.

This elation was short-lived, as I soon discovered what a tyrant my stepfather was. He made it his job to see that I did well in school, and it was under the pretext of helping me with schoolwork that the torture began. Whenever he was bored, he would summon me to his bedroom, where he would be reclining on the bed. He would ask me to fetch one of my textbooks and randomly point out questions for me to answer. Invariably, the pure terror of what was to come would render my mind completely blank. I would stare at the page with despair and fear. If I was lucky, I might overcome my anxiety and manage to get the answer right. But if I was too terrified and couldn't answer the question, he would make me pay.

If he was in a better mood, he would just belt me hard on the small of my back with his two-inch belt, or whip the inside of my outstretched arms with three canes tied together. If he was feeling mean, he would tie my hands behind my back, lift me up by my tied ankles and submerge my head in a large bucket of water that I had to fill up beforehand. The sensation of being drowned is still vivid in my mind; the desperate feeling as my nose sucks in water, the wild thrashing of my upside-down torso against the side of the bucket as my self-preservation instinct goes into overdrive. This would go on for what felt like an eternity. Then, suddenly, the instinctive urge to struggle would stop as a tremendous sense of peace overcame me. I must have been losing consciousness because my body would start to relax, and this would be the exact moment that he lifted my head out of the bucket.

As I spluttered and coughed, my head reeling, I would invariably hear my mother protesting in the background. *"Why don't you just hit her with the cane? You can thump her as much as you like, just don't drown her,"* she would quietly lament. His response was always the same. He would calmly restate the fact that if she interfered, he would have nothing more to do with my education. That retort always shut my mother up instantly.

When she was five, her parents had been taken away one day by so-called freedom fighters, and they never returned. Instead of having an education, she ended up working from a tender age and felt that her quality of life had been vastly compromised because of that. My stepfather knew this was her Achilles heel and would use it to legitimise subjecting me to all kinds of torture. This included telling me to put drawing pins on the floor and insisting I knelt into them. I don't know which was worse, the agony of staring into the pins for what seemed like hours with apprehension and fear, hoping that he would change his mind, or the actual pain when those sharp metal ends sank into my little knees. I only know that, as my knees bled as I pulled out each drawing pin, I always made a silent wish that I would bleed to death to teach him a lesson for being so unkind.

I was super-sensitive to my stepfather's moods whenever he arrived home from work. I could even pick up the vibes from another room because my survival for the day depended upon it. Whenever he wanted to amuse himself, he would hone in on my studies. I was bright at school, but I remember receiving a beating when I couldn't even spell 'able' during one of our tormenting sessions. I now understand how fear can immobilise us and render us ineffective even when faced with the simplest of tasks.

The arrival of my half-brother when I was twelve did not improve the situation at home, but school was my sanctuary. I got on well with the teachers and was bright and chirpy at school, but at home I never uttered a word unless I was spoken to. When I wasn't doing my school work, I was doing the scrubbing, cleaning and cooking, or looking after my brother. Any form of recreation or friendship was out of bounds. Story books were a big no-no too, so I used to sneakily read them under the bed and pretend to be asleep if anyone took a peek at me. I think Enid Blyton saved my sanity. I used to disappear into her enchanting stories and would often hope that I would encounter my own fairy godmother who would grant me my wish – to be the wisest person on the planet!

My stepfather's intentions towards me turned sexual when I was sixteen. As if turned on by a switch, he was now also sweet-talking me in between the beatings. The torture had moved from the physical onto a more mental level. It was the last straw. It took me beyond what I could endure, and forced me to make the most important decision of my life. He intended to divorce my mother and wanted me to be with him. While he was making plans in his head, he called me to his side and said: *"One day, when we're together after I've divorced your mother and you come home from school upset and I come back from the office feeling down and that thing happens, what would you do?"*

The moment those fateful words escaped his lips, a thousand alarm bells went off inside me. Even though I had never even talked to a boy, I knew exactly what he meant by that thing. So far, aside from the beatings, he had not touched me in a sexual way, and I knew that for him to ask me, he must have been thinking about it. I had always looked upon him as a father figure, and the thought of him having sexual designs on my innocent body made me feel nauseous. So I put the worst idea into his head. I told him if that ever happened, I would commit suicide because I wouldn't be able to handle the shame. His response was: *"Oh, I'm glad I asked first."*

From that moment on, I knew I wasn't safe. So, one quiet afternoon while my mother was sitting by the table having her cigarette, I told her what my stepfather had said. Her body was facing away from me, and I remember the long, deliberate silence. When she finally spoke, she said: *"Don't tell anyone"*. And that was it. As I walked away, I knew with absolute clarity that my mother would not be able to help me. I knew I had to save my own life. I had to run away and there was no time to lose. The last week of school was approaching before we broke up for the annual vacation, which meant I would be trapped and not have a legitimate reason to leave the house. The school report was due home that week, and if I had failed in more than two subjects, the punishment would be to stand naked in front of my stepfather as a penance for not knowing shame.

His relationship with my mother had deteriorated so badly that she had been threatening suicide. All this was too much for my young mind to bear. I planned my getaway on the Sunday, borrowed money for the taxi fare on the Monday, and left on the Tuesday.

That morning, the air felt different. Everyone was still asleep when I got dressed, ready for school like any other ordinary morning. But I remember there was lightness in the air, a strange brightness in the morning light that I had never noticed before. It was as if the angels were holding their breath and cheering me on at the same time.

I quietly left the house, and headed for school. As our classroom was being used for the fifth form's national examination that week, we congregated at the school canteen to have our attendance registered. After that, I quietly slipped away and hailed a taxi. I asked the driver to take me to an address that I had kept safe in my head for many years. It was my father's address, which I had visited a couple of times when I was eight. (That was when I had discovered for the first time that I was not alone, and that I had two brothers and a sister.) During the four-hour journey, every time the taxi approached a police checkpoint, my heart would be in my mouth as I remembered the horrific torture that my stepfather had promised to inflict on me if ever I should run away. But I arrived safely at my destination, and my father took me in without a second's hesitation.

I never saw my stepfather or my mother again, except in my nightmares, where they would be chasing me. But the bad dreams stopped the day I found out my mother had died.

What was left of me then was a young girl with extremely low self-esteem and a pessimistic view of life. I couldn't understand why I was still so unhappy, even though I was no longer at the mercy of my stepfather. I thought I would feel free and overjoyed, but the opposite was true. I didn't feel good about myself. I felt I didn't deserve to be happy. There was an inner force that was oppressing me now, repeating the same harsh words that had come from the lips of my mother and my stepfather. *"Look at you, you're so ugly. If you don't do well in your studies, no one will want to marry you!"*

Even though I was now free of my stepfather's tyranny and living in a gentler environment with my father, it did not release me from the grip of the negativity that was now running my inner show. I was withdrawn and had a negative outlook towards life. As I had run away in the fourth grade and didn't have the leaving certificate that I needed to enrol at a new school, I didn't do the fifth grade. I began to think that I wouldn't have a bright future without formal qualifications.

I still remember my father saying to me that an optimist would always look upwards when communicating, while a pessimist would stare towards the ground. How true! At that time, I was definitely more familiar with the lower view. His words made me think, though. Somehow, looking upwards allowed me to access a more optimistic side of myself that I didn't even know was there!

One day, I came across an article by a well-known spiritual teacher with a caption that read: *'Your disposition depends on your point of view'*. The article explained that *how we feel depends on how we look at things*. In other words, if we look at a situation in a negative light, we will experience negative emotions. It went on to explain that our quality of life is completely determined by ourselves, that happiness is ours for the taking, and to find it we simply need to have the right attitudes. Wow! This was just what my pessimistic sixteen-year-old mind needed to hear.

It was my first taste of self-empowerment, and I ran with it. I stuck the article on my bedroom wall and scoured every bookshop I could find for inspirational books. I loved every bit of wisdom I came across. My wounded soul was soothed and comforted by the knowledge that all was not lost, that no matter what had happened to me in the past, I could still decide how I wanted my life to pan out; that I chose the path I walked, and I had the power to manifest my own happiness. There was so much to learn, so much to understand, and so much to experiment with and to put into practice to see if these lofty concepts really worked.

I also began an apprenticeship with my father, a Chinese physician who specialised in setting bones and fixing dislocated joints. For a couple of years, I fixed patients' broken bones whenever my father was on holiday. This was my first training in healing. I also taught myself yoga and even ran a little class with my friends, as they were keen to learn. I was beginning to appreciate that we can play a definitive role in improving and maintaining the health of our body.

Living with my father, who is a wise and knowledgeable man, gave me many opportunities to hear the wisdom teachings that he had found helpful in his life. Being a Buddhist, he explained the law of cause and effect (karma); that we reap from the seeds we have sowed, that each is responsible for his own actions and, because of the precision of this law, no one gets away with anything. We are totally accountable for every deed we have done.

I remember sitting there, stunned by this piece of information. I thought of my stepfather. I thought that if he was accountable for all the violence and cruelty that he had inflicted on me for the previous six years, he had enough to deal with already. He didn't need me to direct my anger towards him and make it worse. I felt compassion for him. I thought the kindest thing was to forgive and set him free from any hatred that might be tempted to rear up in me, especially if I took the victim stance. I also saw that to release him from my own emotions was a kindly act towards myself. After all the hardship I had endured, it made sense to have a more benevolent attitude towards myself.

As my outlook became more positive, I also started to draw in opportunities to excel. I went from the apprenticeship with my father to working for the biggest art supplier in Kuala Lumpur. My boss saw my potential and kept moving me up the ladder, and eventually I came over to England and set up my own retail/wholesale business. I married a man who adored me, and at twenty-eight had everything that we girls were told the fairytale dream was all about.

But I still wasn't happy, and I couldn't understand why. I was shocked that 'having it all' didn't fulfil me. All your life you wait to get to a certain point, thinking that you'll live happily ever after when you get there, but all that was waiting was an anti-climax! That was enough to set me on the quest again. I moved away from the business world and began to study Shiatsu (acupressure). I had no intention of being a Shiatsu practitioner, but I loved the knowledge I received from the course, especially about Chinese Medicine. It came in handy when I eventually taught Tai Chi Qi Gong.

I intensified my learning again, and by now thousands of books were available on every self-help or spiritual topic you could think of. I travelled to learn from many wonderful teachers, I sat and received wisdom from enlightened masters and, most of all, I put into practice what I had learnt and found the teachings incredibly effective and powerful in reshaping my life. I love any spiritual teachings that are practical and that can make an immediate difference in one's life.

The greatest difference I see now is that I love the Juicy person I am. I have become my own greatest ally, and I continue to be thrilled by everyday life. My enthusiasm for all things good and beautiful is inexhaustible, and I love the positive effects it can bring to those around me. Through understanding more about the invisible laws that govern life, I have learnt how to work in harmony with life, as opposed to fighting it. I am now wise enough not to resist anything over which I have no control. The wondrous thing is, when I am not afraid and I am open to seeing the truth, I find that everything has a tremendous gift for me. Trusting this, slowly and surely, I am learning to be a lover of *what is*, which is another name for reality. I now see all things as good, no matter what they look like.

I can't remember the last time I struggled with anything, be it physical, mental or emotional. Life is now sweet and effortless because I have learnt not to believe in the stories my mind tells me. I understand that it is the unquestioned thoughts in my head that cause me to suffer, not life itself! Even when a challenge appears at my door, I now see it as a great opportunity, simply to help me grow fuller into my joy, which is the only growth I'm interested in. Any resistance or aversion I have is only here to show me where I am limiting myself though my own thinking. I love pushing myself beyond these crazy ideas we've been programmed with: *"I can't do this"*, *"Who do I think I am to go for such excellence?"* *"It's too late for me"* *"What difference can one person make?"*

Fear is no longer my god. Love is. I discovered that this Love is more than just an emotion, more than just a special feeling we have towards people we care about, and more than just a romantic notion we have about our beloved. The more I learn about this Love, the more I come to see that it is the very force of life that joins all things into a harmonious whole. And the deeper I delve into the mystery of who I am, who every human being is, and what every living thing is, the clearer it becomes that everyone and everything is a loving strand of this vast tapestry of Love, only we are not aware of it.

Now I have no doubt that this Love is the spiritual essence of who we are. I have arrived at a place inside me where Love is synonymous to God. The power of transformation that comes from this place still awes me to no end. The vast healing that pours out of it still humbles me, when I am quiet enough to see it. And I know that every single human being has this inside too. In this inner place, all suffering—be it mental, emotional or physical—stops, and bliss begins.

The more I learn about the wisdom of life, the more I can see that my horrendous childhood was in fact a blessing, a gift for a greater purpose. For many years now, I have regarded my stepfather as one of my greatest teachers. I still feel tremendous compassion towards him. While I have benefited from the whole experience, he is still held accountable for being the 'bad guy' in my life. He is no longer here, but I only have love and gratitude towards him. I'm glad I visited him a few months before he died, so that he knew I felt no malice towards him.

As for my mother, who didn't give me the love and affection I was hungry for, or manage to protect me from the cruelty of my stepfather, I know she did the best she knew how. Her own childhood was very sad and horrendous too, and I'm sure she loved me in her own way, even though I never experienced this softness from her. It was only when I became a mother myself that I was aware of the intense maternal instinct we have to protect our offspring. To watch her daughter being subjected to such cruelty must have been devastating for her. And to not be able to rescue me from it must have riddled her with guilt. She may not be physically in this world any more, but I love her and she lives on in me. I'm grateful to her for bringing me into the world and for playing a part in shaping the person I am now. It is not in *spite* of my childhood, it is *through* my childhood that I am who I am today.

Now, when I sit with people who have been through similar 'atrocities' and feel too bruised and battered to pick themselves up again, I can help them believe that if I can do it, so can they. It has given me the belief to say to them with utter conviction that their past experience doesn't have to break them. They can use it to rise out of the ashes.

For the past sixteen years, I have been teaching self-empowerment and spiritual courses. I have seen miracles take place. I have watched depressed women with suicidal tendencies heal and move on to enjoy their life. I have seen relationships heal and become a vehicle of joy for couples who thought they couldn't live together any more. I have seen women with 'caterpillar' attitudes take this inner journey and emerge as beautiful butterflies. I know everything is possible for the open mind, and that we all have the potential to unleash the JuicyWoman within us. I would love to share this wonderful and kind reality with anyone who wants the same.

With Joy and Blessings
Ocean WhiteHawk
Mother's Day March 2009

A Juicy Perspective

This book *JuicyWoman* brings a holy vision. This vision is about every woman bringing her deepest dream to life. It is about you feeling so complete within yourself because you are living the truth of who you are: the radiance of Love, the living force of the universe. What makes you the radiance of Love is the light that shines out of you when you're truly happy. You are truly happy when you are being who you are. This light uplifts and inspires. What makes you the living force of the universe is that when you're happy, your presence heals. And when you no longer hide behind the conditioned belief that you are less than brilliant and begin to live as this powerful Love-force, the chance of the world becoming a better place will increase ten thousand-fold.

To heed this vision, you cannot say you have no time, because you are too busy holding down a job, with children to feed or a husband to look after. You cannot say you can't do it because you don't want to hurt those close to you. You cannot say you are not living your dream because your man won't let you.

Instead you need to be bold, to go beyond the edges of your fears. You need to have courage and jump from the precipice of the known, the familiar, into the great unknown, where your infinite potential awaits you. You also need to be prepared to die to the old, so that the glorious new can be reborn inside you. This means you will challenge every belief you have about who you think you are. This also means you are willing to move out of your comfort zone to discover the unexplored landscapes within your own psyche. Then, and only then will you earn the right to meet this truly astonishing woman in you.

You need to do all these things because life needs you, like nature needs the earth. Life needs women to collectively find a new way, a more loving and gentler way because too many things are not working out for us. This disharmony in life is mirrored in the health issues we struggle with, from constant migraines and bad back to the ever increasing breast cancer. Our stress level has rocketed to the moon ever since we started to bring money to the table and many of us are more tired than ever. For many, day to day living is no longer a big love affair. There is a real urgency to return to the delicious joy that lies waiting in our very own heart. The power to do so is within you. All you need do is to leave the lap of fear and return to the waiting arms of Love inside you. And this book will help you to do just that.

Your Juicy Essence

*Every woman
is more amazing
than she believes
or has ever been led to believe.*

1

The JuicyWoman in You

'Juicy' conjures up a mouth-watering image, of luscious nectar spreading over our sweet lips as we sink into the soft moist flesh of a delicious fruit. The term 'Juicy Woman' might suggest a woman who is a bit saucy, and it is often used in a tongue-in-cheek fashion.

But the JuicyWoman we are talking about here is much more than that. She is the root of who you are, your unchanging presence in the face of change. She is the radical self in every woman; the being in you that remains unaffected, unaltered, no matter what the personality goes through. This JuicyWoman in you is not shaped by life out there. Life is transient and she is not. She remains when all else falls away.

A JuicyWoman is *in* the world but definitely not *of* the world. She functions in the world with great ease and sees all occurrences, all happenings as blessings because she sees beyond appearances. She is your undomesticated self, raw in energy and unlimited in power and potential. When you place her at the helm of your life, you won't have a past to regret, or a future to worry about. You will see your life perfect as it is, while being open and ever ready for miracle upon miracle to unfold in front of you in each spontaneous moment.

She is the woman in you that is beyond being wife, mother, daughter, sister or any other roles you may play. She does not hide behind duty or domesticity. She does not hide behind her career or her busyness. She may cook, wash, earn the cash and feed the children, but in the silence of the night and depths of her soul, she knows who she is. This part of us has never been tamed. Always innocent, totally natural, she puzzles at the contrived political correctness, and the game of false pretences that humans sometimes play. And when we are not being true to our self, she is furthest away from us.

The JuicyWoman in every woman is beautiful beyond her wildest imagination. At each moment, she is perfectly designed, each line and tone of colour precise, without a speck out of place. Whether her thighs are fat or thin, whether her breasts are large or small, whether her skin is dewy smooth or cheerfully wrinkled, she is still gorgeous. She only needs to feel this truth for her inborn beauty to be obvious to her.

This JuicyWoman in each of us is now demanding to be born into our everyday life, imploring us to be happy with who we are and what we have. How can we tell? When we stop and look, not just with our ordinary eyes, but with the stillness of mind, the signs are pretty obvious. Here are some of them.

- Each time you suffer physically, mentally or emotionally. Whether you're having an identity crisis because you've been made redundant from your high-powered job, you are not able to have the child your maternal arms long to hold, or you are feeling utterly rejected because your man has decided to move on—these traumas can be alleviated by getting in touch with the juiciness within you. Each moment of pain is simply an invitation to be this wondrous creature that you already are, even though you may not know it.

- Every moment you are at war with yourself, feeling guilty, feeling shame, feeling not good enough, it is because you have forgotten your Juicy essence, which is your Love nature. Experiencing spiritual amnesia, you doubt the vast potential that is within you and suffer the discomfort of squeezing your infinite self into this tiny, superficial, make-believe identity called 'I'.

- Every time you struggle, in your relationship or work, with friends or family, it is because you have not awakened to the power of Love inside you. Feeling disempowered, you struggle in relationships with others because you believe you need their love, approval or acceptance to validate you. This is painful because nobody can give you what you must give to yourself.

- Each instant you are in conflict with reality, not accepting what is, arguing for what is not, you put yourself through stress and anxiety. Your distress is not caused by what is happening, but because you have yet to recognise the blessing every situation brings. This is due to the lack of spiritual insight that is naturally present when your JuicyWoman awakens.

But let's get one thing straight. There can be no JuicyWoman without the spiritual self. In fact, your JuicyWoman is your spiritual self. Your juiciness can only be drawn from the well of your spiritual source, Love, every hour, every day. Some of us may name this source God, while some of us may be more comfortable with the term Human Goodness. Whatever name we give it, or none at all, it matters not. What matters is that you wake up to the fact that you are a Love being, as opposed to just an ordinary human being. This Love self is your spiritual self, the truth of who you are. Any other identity is simply the superficial self, a substitute the mind has invented in the name of survival.

The quicker you become aware of this Juicy self, the easier and sweeter your life will be. You are this Love self, even if you don't believe it. It doesn't matter how hard you try to disconnect from this real you, it is not possible. You are that, whether you like it or not. That's the good news. The not-so-good news is that when you are not aware of this true you, you suffer. Stress is the experience of this self-forgetting; external circumstances will seem to affect you or have a hold over your sanity. If you want to be kind to yourself, you won't delay this inner journey to the timeless wisdom inside you. The first step to this wondrous journey is to open your beautiful mind and read on.

A JuicyWoman does not waste time in resisting the good stuff just because certain details don't match her own ideas. Mind opened wide, heart willing and receptive to whatever comes her way, she dives into the ocean of life and emerges as a precious pearl, more luscious and more brilliant than ever.

If you are constantly tired,
uninspired,
and feel overwhelmed by things that need to be done,
it's not because you have too much on your plate,
or not enough time to do them.
It's because you have forgotten
the most essential element in your life
- YOU.

2

Do You Recognise Yourself in any of This?

- stressed woman?
- frustrated woman?
- unhappy woman?
- confused woman?
- unappreciated woman?
- lonely woman?
- tired woman?
- fearful woman?
- unloved woman?
- disheartened woman?
- unfulfilled woman?
- exhausted woman?

- unseen woman?
- disillusioned woman?
- forgotten woman?
- humiliated woman?
- stifled woman?
- 'doormat' woman?
- abused woman?
- desperate woman?
- crushed woman?
- lost woman?
- downtrodden woman?

Bad news: *If you find yourself saying yes to the any of the above on a regular basis, it means you have essentially neglected yourself. Disconnected from your JuicyWoman, you feel a victim of external circumstances. Until you do something about your life, your misery will keep on.*

Good news: *If you are willing to open your mind, to give attention and the commitment needed to overhaul your out-of-date thinking, your life will change for the better. Boldness of heart and dedication is required to come home to your Juicy self.*

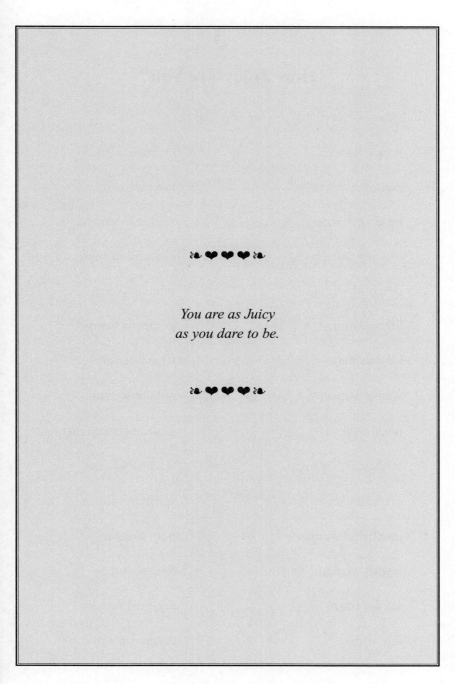

❧ ❤ ❤ ❤ ❧

You are as Juicy
as you dare to be.

❧ ❤ ❤ ❤ ❧

3

How Juicy are You?

Tick the hearts you think you are and find out.

♡ happy woman	♡ creative woman
♡ confident woman	♡ bold woman
♡ healthy woman	♡ sensuous woman
♡ trusting woman	♡ graceful woman
♡ peaceful woman	♡ vibrant woman
♡ loving woman	♡ gorgeous woman
♡ kind woman	♡ wise woman
♡ strong woman	♡ radiant woman
♡ loved woman	♡ innovative woman
♡ affectionate woman	♡ fearless woman
♡ grateful woman	♡ spiritual woman
♡ intelligent woman	♡ holy woman
♡ joyous woman	♡ oracle woman
♡ sexy woman	♡ mystical woman
♡ fun woman	♡ divine woman

Less than 15:   *You feel that life has squeezed the juiciness out of you. Sparkle and deep joy are alien concepts to you as you spend quite a bit of your time treading water. Sometimes you have a feeling that there is more in you but you don't know how to get it out. Fear stops you from venturing out of your comfort zone to find the edges of your excellence.*

Less than 25:   *You feel better than the average woman and enjoy life to a larger degree than most. If you dare to take that quantum leap, you're there!*

25 or more: *You are definitely a JuicyWoman. The world is your oyster and life is one continuous dance of delight for you. You are a shining example and inspiration for all women.*

❧ ♥ ♥ ♥ ❧

As Life kisses her
she wakes up
to who she truly is.
From this day on
she lives happily ever after.

❧ ♥ ♥ ♥ ❧

4

Unhelpful Fairytales

How did we come to forget all those wonderful juicy qualities in us? What has caused this sickness of self-forgetting? To understand this, we need to look at the psychological food fed to us while we were still innocently running around in our pigtails. And we need to look no further than fairytales.

Every little girl loves her fairytales. The stories all seem so innocent, so romantic, polished with an idealistic shine. Girl *always* meets handsome young prince and *always* lives happily ever after. But parents didn't know fairytales were toxic to our psyche. How they would distort healthy ideas of our female capabilities to achieve happiness, inner strength and wisdom through our own merits.

When we digest the idea that first of all we need rescuing, we are off to a bad start. Our young minds begin to see women as weak and helpless souls, unable to save their own skin. The only way out is a handsome prince on a white horse. In fact, that seems to be the *only* way she will be able to live happily ever after! The overall message in a typical fairytale is this: you haven't got a life unless a prince comes along.

How many white horses do you ever get to see in reality? And how many handsome princes are there, lurking around waiting to kiss you? Have you noticed how many unhappy women there are on this planet right now? Wake up, sleeping beauties of this world, it is time to change the story of your life! You have no choice because you are not going to find your prince by staying asleep. You can spend another five years chasing around in the speed dating stables, but you ain't gonna find your prince that way. Hanging around with girlfriends who have loser attitudes, blaming everything out there but themselves for their misdemeanours in life, won't work either. Lamenting what bastards men are, or thinking that all the good ones have been taken already, will not get you your castle or your knight.

This is what the awakened JuicyWoman in you will do. She will leap off that ivory tower of self-imprisonment and realise that she can fly. The only reason you don't know you have wings is because you have never bothered to try them out or have been told that wings only belonged to feathered-ones or the realms of angels. So all these years you've put up with damp castle walls and deep loneliness for nothing!

What they didn't tell you in fairytales is that you have your own kingdom. And that from the moment you were created, you were given all the powers needed to command a wondrous life for yourself and all those around you. While you have been waiting for the man to show up and lead you to his castle, you have completely neglected your own treasures. Come home. Start to investigate and question your mind. Everything you need for a deep, fulfilled life lies waiting behind the veil of your confused thoughts. Everything you ever wanted is inside you all along, waiting for you to claim it.

Here's the sting in the tail. Most fairytales were actually written by men. *Cinderella, The Frog Prince, Rapunzel* and many others were written by… wait for it… THE BROTHERS GRIMM!! We should have guessed.

A JuicyWoman would detox fairytales out of her psyche as it is not realistic to expect a man to know what her deepest dream is, never mind the way to get to it. Our deepest dream is not to have the fairytale. Our deepest dream is to be who we are. Sweet and wonderful as men may be, they can't possibly teach us what we need to know about being a true woman, an honest authentic female who truly knows what makes her heart sing.

ዮ ❤ ❤ ❤ ዮ

And she saw that every woman
was herself.
And if she stabbed her sister
her own heart would bleed profusely.
And when she loved her sister
her own heart would take winged flight.

ዮ ❤ ❤ ❤ ዮ

5

Despising Our Own Kind

In fairytales, a young girl's mind is bombarded by the ugly witch, the wicked stepmother, the cruel queen, the old hag, the ice queen, the ugly sisters, Cruella, and on and on it goes. Even in the Bible, Eve is responsible for her and Adam being chucked out of the Garden of Eden! Take a good look and you will notice that most of the stories that we grow up with are riddled with negative archetypes of women. As if that doesn't damage our psyche enough, the victim is usually an innocent little girl. So both the villain and the victim are female! What do we learn from these seemingly innocent stories? That we are the baddies as well as the victims. We can't win either way.

But what harm can innocent stories like these do, you might ask. To understand this, we need to look at this marvellous mind we have. This amazing piece of kit has two aspects: the conscious and the subconscious. Your conscious mind, the mind that is concentrating on reading right now, processes approximately two thousand bits of information per second. Pretty good going. But that's small potatoes when compared to the goliath of your subconscious mind, which can process up to four billion bits per second! The figures may vary slightly depending on the scientific source, but one thing is crystal clear – your subconscious mind is shockingly more powerful than your ordinary conscious mind.

The conscious mind deals with the present, while the subconscious records and stores every experience and impression you have received from the moment of conception, good and bad alike. If your parents constantly argue and fight in their relationship, you will have an unconscious expectation to do the same in your relationships, unless you make a conscious effort not to. Or you might go the other way and avoid confrontation altogether. A mother who has body weight issues will invariably pass them on to her daughters without meaning to. Each time a young girl watches her mother display hang-ups about wrinkles, ageing or her body image, she absorbs the same patterns into herself by osmosis! Basically, whatever your mind is exposed to on a regular basis forms a kind of psychic blueprint in your subconscious that repeats the same expectation in you. That is why we find ourselves repeating with our children the same abhorrent patterns our parents dished out on us.

We are also constantly being fed a diet by the media of stories and images of how women should look. Being thin is good, and if we dress well, even better. So we subconsciously become judgemental about those who are overweight, and if their fashion sense isn't up to scratch, they fall off our radar altogether. We home in on their 'imperfections' because it distracts us from our judgement of our own perceived imperfections. It makes us feel momentarily better.

Ninety-five percent of our waking time is dominated by the subconscious mind. Unless you have trained your mind to be alert to all your internal patterns, which takes a high level of awareness, one that needs to be carefully trained over years, most of the time you are simply playing out these patterns without realising that you are doing so. It is said that from birth to the age of seven, we take in the data. The computer mind is being programmed. After that, we spend the rest of our life using all the stored information as reference points for whatever we do. The grave news is that unless we make a point of deleting the negative programmes and installing new, positive ones, we will continue to experience the same pitfalls.

So feeding pliable young minds with stories that depict women in a negative light is not good for our female psyche. In fairytales, we get the message that ugly sisters and wicked stepmothers can prevent us from getting to the ball of our life. We learn that jealous women are willing to sentence us to death because we are more beautiful than they are. We subconsciously draw the conclusion that women are she-devils and that they will do anything to stand in the way of our happiness.

Nowadays, we have women who would stop at nothing to steal our man away for themselves. We have our sisters bitching about us behind our back. We even have women who will go to any lengths to seduce our beloved, not because they want him, but simply to be spiteful. This is an illness we need to heal. We have come to despise our own kind because of this deep mistrust that began as innocent stories in fairytales. Women became threats rather than supportive allies of true sisterhood. The fact that you are a woman yourself creates an extra tension in your psyche, an unfortunate double whammy. Inside us we have *women are not to be trusted* sitting side-by-side with *I am also a woman*. This creates a conflicting inner current, which in extreme cases can generate an unconscious mistrust and hatred towards ourself and our own kind. This is so subtle that often we are not aware that it is there. Look harder and you will see how true this is.

Most seemingly innocent fairytales and childhood stories have subtly poisoned our mind into believing we are the victims and the villains in the story of our life. We must heal this lie if we are to live happily ever after. We can do this, and we must. We need new wonder stories that portray Woman in her true, life-giving light.

We begin by changing the lens through which we look at ourselves. We concentrate on and highlight not only our outer assets but, more importantly, our gracious inner ones. Do we appreciate what a wonderful woman we are, and the mere fact that we laugh, we cry and our arms are always ready to embrace all who need a good hug? Once we have established self-appreciation, the critical lens through which we used to look will naturally fall away, and there will be more kindness in the way we see our sisters. Using a soft-focus lens, we will home in on the warmth of their smile, on the generosity of their nature and the delightful openness of their feminine heart. We will start to notice how amazing it is to be a woman, and how our world is filled with so many lovely women, touching our heart and sweetening our day.

A JuicyWoman is a woman who allows herself to be inspired by all great women, dead or alive, in myths or in legends. She knows that every noble woman is simply a silent reminder that her own exaltation lies waiting within. Because she trusts her own kind, she flourishes into her own fullness. She loves being a woman and she loves women, finding a sister in each one. She notices that she is frequently being touched by the beauty and kindness of women in her everyday life.

My father didn't love me,
not because I was unlovable.
It was because he didn't love himself.

My father hurt me,
not because I deserved it.
It was because he was hurting inside.

My father left me,
not because I was unimportant to him.
It was because he couldn't stay with himself.

6

Is Your Father/Daughter Relationship Wounded?

When we were children, our parents were our gods. Their influence upon us shapes our human make-up, for better or for worse. As daughters growing up, our emotional and spiritual growth is deeply affected by our relationship with our father. He is the first masculine figure in our life, and he plays a key role in shaping the way we relate to the masculine side of our nature and, ultimately, to all the men in our life. Our relationship with our father is pivotal to our subsequent relationship with every man who enters into our life thereafter. And the way he relates to our femininity affects the way we grow into womanhood. The result can be a self-assured, confident woman who likes herself and enjoys her femininity, or, at the opposite end of the scale, a weak-willed woman who doesn't believe in her own capabilities and feels inferior.

If you grow up with a father who constantly affirms to you that you are beautiful, that you deserve to be treated with love, respect and dignity, and that women are wonderful creatures, the chances are you will have a healthy expectation that the men in your life treat you in a similar manner. You will probably feel good about yourself, glow with self-esteem and enjoy being a woman. You will value the worth of being feminine.

But if you grow up with an authoritarian father, and a mother who is passively dependent while he dominates both you and her, there is a strong chance that you will find it difficult to achieve genuine feminine independence in your life. You will end up with a man not unlike your rigid father, who tells you what to do while he takes care of your physical needs. Such a man is not in touch with his feminine side and is likely to squash your soft, emotional nature. If you have chosen to rebel against your father's authority, it could be out of a defensive reaction against patriarchal authority, rather than out of your own feminine needs and values. You will probably end up being with a man who is more effeminate in nature, perhaps more placid than you are, so that you won't need to feel threatened by his male authority.

If you had an absent father or a negligent father, you are more than likely to compensate for this by armouring yourself and building up a strong masculine ego identity through achievement or being an activist – fighting for some kind of 'worthy' cause. Being in control is a big thing for you. Since your father didn't give you what you needed, you have this steely determination to do it yourself. But this tough masculine identity is often a mask to anaesthetise against the pain of abandonment or rejection by your father. Unfortunately, this seemingly strong and tough exterior also blocks you from your own feminine feelings and soft side. Beneath the veneer of success and contentment lie the wounded self, the hidden despair, the feelings of loneliness and isolation, the tears and the rage. Deep down, you are terrified of being vulnerable.

You may have a need to lay down the law in your relationship to cover up your own fears of abandonment. If you have this tendency, you need to see that control is a false strength and will not work in the long run. Your growth would be to learn to trust and surrender into the openness of Love, of what is, rather than what you think it should be. There may also be a subconscious expectation for men to reject or leave you. Consciously, you may not be aware of it, but lurking in the dark recesses of your mind is a fear that he might leave you. You may even develop a pattern of being the one to leave a relationship to avoid the pain of being left by the man.

This absent father syndrome can often be the reason why many successful women have unsuccessful relationships. They either find it hard to attract the right partner, or find long-term relationships difficult. On the outer level, they are accomplished in their fields, financially independent and self-sufficient. They seem secure and confident, powerful and strong on the outside. But on the inside, feelings of weariness and exhaustion overwhelm them from time to time, and a deep loneliness gnaws away at an unmet heart. And until a woman heals this inner wounding of the father/daughter relationship, she runs the risk of spending the rest of her days without ever meeting her true beloved.

Many of us suffer from a wounded relationship with this paternal figure. The roots of the father-daughter wound are deep and penetrate right through to the core of our psychological and emotional make-up. This dysfunction even shows in our body. It can become overwhelmed by disease. It becomes rigid, inflexible and unyielding. It is as if we have encased our body in psychic iron bars. We lose the graceful flow in our body, the fundamental aspect of our feminine beauty. Not flowing, we stop glowing as well. The light that we are stops shining, dulled by the festering wound of an unhealed father-daughter relationship.

Our feminine side is the part of us that dreams and holds the vision of our life. And it is our masculine side that manifests this vision, in an active and dynamic way. The good news is that although a woman may be wounded from an impaired relationship with her father, it is possible for her to work towards healing this wound to her masculine side. We may bear the influences of our parents, but ultimately we are more than just the product of our parents. There is a spiritual drive in the psyche that compels us towards balance and wholeness, a sort of natural healing process. Some of us move towards this goal because we are fed-up with having failed relationships and an unfulfilled life. Others choose to heal because the pain is too much to bear. And there are those who resist and are dragged kicking and screaming, for it is the soul's innate nature to grow, whether we like it or not.

To heal, first we must accept that what has happened was meant to be. It was meant to be not because life is unkind and wishes for us to suffer, but for the growth that comes out of it when we stop seeing ourselves or someone else as a victim. Each of us, including our perceived 'perpetrator', has done, is doing and will always do the best we know how in any given moment. Our best might not measure up to someone else's best, but it is our best all the same. Our compassionate heart will see that each of us has always done what we believed to be the right thing at the time. And that we can only be true to the moment. When we can embrace what has happened, we are ready to forgive and let go. Healing automatically takes place when we do that. If we have a gap where we feel a father-figure is missing, we can lovingly fill it by getting in touch with our inner masculine. This means becoming aware that we have an aspect in us that can direct and protect our feminine soul whenever needed. And the rest of the time, we can be happy to lounge softly in our openness, which is a powerful trait of our femininity, and to enjoy the ease that it brings, especially in our relationship with our beloved.

A JuicyWoman realises that until she heals the wound in the father-daughter relationship, the psychic pus from this wound will contaminate her relationship with all the men in her life. It will also limit the power and ability of her masculine side, compromising her effectiveness to manifest what she wants in her life. She needs to understand the wound and identify what has been lacking, so that it can be developed from within. Once the injury is understood, that very wound needs to be accepted on a total level, for it is only through acceptance that healing and compassion can arise, both for her and for her father. And for their relationship.

There is no life
without Woman.

7

The Incredible Power of the Feminine

Woman shapes the world.

It is Woman who gives birth to *every* man, woman, and child you see. Without Woman, there would be no human species on this planet. Sperms may be frozen to fertilise eggs, but there will be no babies without Woman to gestate new life in her precious womb. As a woman, take a moment right now, breathe into your juicy belly and *feel* this awesome fact. Gently appreciate how amazing it is to be a woman.

With a few exceptions, Woman also moulds every human being on this planet before he or she is released into life. Up until the last few decades, our full-time job was to knead, shape and sculpt our children, to prepare and equip them for the feast of living. Okay, we know this scenario has changed quite a bit, now that we are muscling in with our man to pay the mortgage and put food on the table, but mothers are still primary carers, especially for the first ten years, the vital period when most of the psychic programming takes place. Our daily influence and interactions with our child play a fundamental part in the person they become.

So, if we don't like the look of the world out there, we, women collectively, are partly responsible for it. We may not have directly caused the disharmony and war out there but it's important we see that perhaps by not being in touch with the true potential of who we are as women, it has compromised our influence on the world. By not believing in our innate power to heal and nurture everything that crosses our path, and by being frightened ourselves, we have contributed to the confusion and disarray around us. We must stop blaming men, the government, society, our neighbours or anyone else for that matter for the way the world is.

To take responsibility is the most empowering thing. To own up also means we can make amends and move on. Nobody will beat us with a big stick just because we've messed up. To pretend it has nothing to do with us is to give away our power. In that moment, we are doomed, back to the illusion that we are the weaker gender. Back to untruths like *'men rule the world, so there's nothing I can do about life out there'* or *'what difference can one person make?'* Lies hurt and we suffer. Truth sets us free, free to take notice and do something about it.

So we have helped shaped the world as it is. Knowing that we yield so much power in our hands, we can set out to make things right again. The first place we need to apply this power is in ourselves. The first world you sort out is your own. Does peace reign in your inner world? Or do you attack yourself whenever you feel you don't measure up? Are you gentle and kind with your own soul? Or do you neglect the sound of your own screaming heart? Are you honest with who you are? Or do you pretend to be something else and cheat the world from delighting in the real you? Be the walking peace. Be the talking kindness. Be the living joy. The world will follow. Such immensity is this God-given feminine power.

Responsibility is our ability to respond to what needs Love right now. We need our Love and so does the world.

JuicyWoman is relieved to know that it is not by chance that the world is the way it is – that there is an intelligent order in this seemingly chaotic universe. She now knows that every action of hers counts in designing the world she lives in. With vigour and excitement she can go back to the drawing board and practise her masterstrokes with a masterpiece of a life in mind. Already, the world looks different.

❧ ❤ ❤ ❤ ❧

I am my own authority.
My gift to life is to be who I am,
not who others think I should be.

❧ ❤ ❤ ❤ ❧

8

The Juicy Queen on the Chessboard

Did you know that the queen is the most versatile piece on the chessboard? She can move in all directions and for as many spaces as she likes to guard her king. And what's more, if you lose your queen, when your pawn reaches your opponent's end, the queen is reborn! She resurrects herself through a *'chess-man of smallest size and value'* (that's an Oxford English Dictionary definition!).

Contrary to belief, women are not the weaker sex. They are the *softer* sex. The yielding power in a woman is like the power of water. Water wears down even the hardest of rock. Nothing can stand in its way. Whatever it is, water will flow over it, under it, around it, and, eventually, through it! It's fluidity is its strength.

So, soft yet powerful woman, you cannot be stopped from following what you know to be true. Nobody can stand in your way if you don't allow it. No obstacles can stop you from climbing to the summit of your joy unless you believe it's possible to be obstructed. The moment you believe something outside has power over you, then you have just handed over your authority. The greatest obstacle isn't in your partner, your family or your boss. It's in your own mind: a story you hide behind because you are too terrified to take the chance, lest you might fail. Or you are afraid to shine, to let the world see your glory, because then you'll have to acknowledge your light to yourself.

As the error is in your own mind, there is nothing to fight or change on the outside. Just align your thoughts to *I am my own authority. My gift to life is to be who I am, not who others think I should be.* Then smile, take a deep breath, soften your belly and continue to flow onwards to where your heart is calling. Wondrousness awaits you there.

Just like the queen on the chessboard, no matter how hard life seems to hit you, you don't die. All challenges are simply for the preparing of your majestic self. A diamond needs to be cut before it can shine forth its brilliance.

Never believe in the story of death. There can be no death without rebirth. What is death to a caterpillar? Emergence to a butterfly. What is death to a man called Jesus? Resurrection to his Christ self. You are the same because Love made you the same. Any story that says otherwise is just a figment of your imagination.

Regardless of what life throws at her, the chess Queen reminds JuicyWoman of her own tenacious will to live. Even death cannot stop her. She is the untamed woman in all of us who refuses to lie down and die – no matter what. Her quiet resilience to overcome all awaits every challenge life brings. At each strike, she rises stronger than before. With each blow, only the shackles come apart. Every fire she goes through, she emerges transformed.

৵ ❤ ❤ ❤ ৵

Another woman's glory
is my own glory.

৵ ❤ ❤ ❤ ৵

9

Your Subconscious Beliefs about Woman

It isn't possible to truly understand what being a woman is all about without being aware of your deep subconscious beliefs about women. We take for granted the concept of being a woman. We have assumed that just because we are born girls, it means we know how to grow into a true embodiment of femininity. Wrong. We only have to take a quick look around us to see that, collectively, most women are still struggling to live their joy and ecstasy. We have come this far with our feminine rights to claim a bigger share of the pie, but we are not happier people. Contentment and deep fulfilment still elude most of us. This lack of understanding of our own kind is costing us our true purpose and our rightful bliss.

Un-investigated subconscious beliefs about Woman not only affect the way we relate to women in our life, but crucially, they form the blueprint from which we become the woman we are. In other words, your subconscious beliefs about women, be they positive or negative, determine the kind of woman you are.

The women we grew up with by our side are our biggest role models. They make the deepest imprint in our psyche. If we watch our mother suffer in silence while our drunken father bashes her about, our young mind will conclude that *women are powerless against men*. Our mother might even blame herself for marrying 'the wrong man'. So we learn not only to accept the abuse dished out to us, but we also believe it's our fault for being there in the first place. We feel that we deserve to be punished. Our mind normalises the violence and subconsciously sees it as part of life. And if the same happens to us in our adult life, we think it's the norm.

A girl watching her single mother exhaust herself bringing up the family may conclude that a woman needs to do it all on her own, and that *women can't count on their men folk for support.*

So what other subconscious beliefs do we hold about women? Watch what comes out of women's lips. The message is clear if we look.

Statement: "She is such a bitch. She will do anything to get what she wants"

Belief: *Woman has no integrity.*

Statement: "You can never trust another woman with your man"

Belief: *Woman will betray another woman to get what she wants.*

Statement: "She is miserable and frustrated because of her husband"

Belief: *Woman is at the mercy of a man's behaviour.*

Statement: "Look at her, Little Miss Have-it-all. She thinks she's so special"

Belief: *All women are my rivals in my quest for happiness and success.*

The media also gives us no end of examples of badly behaved women. No wonder our view towards our sisters is often poisoned with suspicion, jealousy and unkindness. The more we think that, the more we seem to attract such women into our life. We need to break this nasty spell. For the healing of every woman, for her feminine goodness to be more available to the world, each woman must make an effort to change the way she looks at her own kind. We must question the old stories in our head and see that having negative beliefs about Woman is self-destructive. And having positive ones will nurture the goodness out of our sisters and our own self.

A JuicyWoman is a cheerleader for all women. Another woman's glory is her own glory so she does not need to be jealous. And if you meet her, she doesn't compromise her joy because you happen to feel down. She doesn't play small because it might make you feel more comfortable. She knows that by staying bright and joyous, your own joy and light is more likely to bounce back from the mirror of who she is.

❧ ❤ ❤ ❤ ❧

If we want to be like men,
to compete, to battle, to be top bitch,
then feminism hasn't gone far enough.

But if we want be ravished in love,
to live and die in brilliant love,
then feminism has gone too far.

❧ ❤ ❤ ❤ ❧

10

Feminism – Have We Gone Too Far?

We have come a long way in the last two thousand years. Our predecessors marched in their long gowns and went on hunger strikes so that we could have the right to vote. These courageous women shed blood so that we could have the right to education. They fought and stood up against our dear men so that we could have the right to inheritance. Throughout the decades, women of all ages have continued to battle for the right to be in high-powered jobs, the right to contraception and birth control, and the right to sexual freedom. As we land our pretty butts in the twenty-first century, we are still fighting: fighting to be the same. Whatever our menfolk have, we want it too. Our female spirit is not appeased that religion still prohibits women from teaching and being spiritual leaders in many parts of the world. And our sensitive body screams at the brutality of female genital mutilation.

We pay tribute to these great warrior women who took to the battleground to give us the freedom women now have. We are thankful that we have come this far. But we must now question if this fighting stance is still valid, if it actually brings us the results we want, or if this aggressive way is moving us further away from happiness? Perhaps it is time to move on to a more graceful way of achieving what our feminine soul longs for.

Let's be honest and take stock of the loss and damage this 'fight for equality' has brought. We see tired and exhausted women everywhere. They struggle to balance career with family life as they rush from board meetings to school runs, sticking ready meals in the oven to feed their flock before finally collapsing into a heap of tiredness at night. We see frustrated women face parenthood on their own, disorientated by having to be mother and father at the same time. And as time goes by, we see more and more lonely women with striking careers and fat bank accounts but no beloved by their side.

Men are confused and are no longer sure what women want from them. We keep sending them non-verbal messages that we don't need them now that we can pay the mortgage and buy frozen sperm.

We also take offence when they offer to take a heavy load off our hands. We see their help as an insinuation that we are weak, so we grip onto the weighty bag for dear life, silently shouting, *"If you can do it, so can I!"*

We insist on 'going dutch' because we don't want to owe him any favours when it would have pleased him to treat us like a lady. We could have enjoyed revelling in our sweet femininity while he indulged us with elegance and charm.

Because men can be lads and misbehave, we feel we can be 'ladettes' too and join them in crude behaviour. We think nothing of getting drunk and flashing our boobs in public. Then we are surprised and hurt when men treat us with disdain. Most of you may not personally behave like this, but as long as there is one woman out there who does, it affects every woman on this planet – such is the law of oneness. It shapes how men treat women as a whole. Rather than turn our back and think that what happens to another woman has nothing to do with us, we need to join hearts and start caring. *All for one and one for all* shall our motto be. This is the potent way to advance feminism from now on – not fight our brothers, but help our sisters instead.

A JuicyWoman is a true feminist. In fact, she's not a feminist at all – she's a womanist. A womanist believes in the goodness of Woman without attacking the ways of Man. She knows that no man can underrate her because she doesn't underrate herself. A true womanist loves men as much as she loves her own womanhood. She allows men to be men and women to be women because only then can these two halves join as one and the most beautiful dance can begin.

&a. ❤ ❤ ❤ &a.

Who am I
when I'm not the wife
when I'm not the mother
when I'm not any of the roles I play?

Who am I
when I stand naked
beyond the thoughts in my head,
when I am alone with myself?

&a. ❤ ❤ ❤ &a.

11

You Are More than The Roles You Play

Women are very good at multi-tasking. Scientific evidence shows that our brain is organised differently to that of a man. To this highly developed skill, add several large heaps of genuine concern for others. Give that a good mix. Then stir in generous helpings of martyrdom and put this mixture into a large baking tin of low self-esteem, stick it in the oven of life and bake it for a few decades. Voila! What you get is an exhausted woman who has forgotten about herself. But she can't stop because there are mouths to feed, jobs to attend to and a mortgage to pay.

Being wife, mother, daughter, sister, friend, colleague, and so on, soaks up most of our attention like a greedy sponge. We take on these roles because that is what we do in life. In fact, most of the time we don't even think about it. We have no time to. From the moment we arise from the horizontal position, we are on the treadmill of fulfilling these roles. We end up so tightly wrapped by these demanding roles, like layer upon layer of clingfilm around our soft soul, that it chokes the living joy out of us. We look in the mirror, and we sort of see the 'me' beneath the sheets of soft clear plastic, but our passion can no longer breathe. In severe cases, the cancerous growth of self-denigration spreads all over and we no longer recognise the woman looking back at us from the mirror.

Many women have become so ingrained in the roles they play that they have lost touch with what they want, and they don't think it's possible for their life to be any different to how it is. It takes a lot of letting go, of limiting beliefs and fear, before they can entertain the idea of going back to the drawing board and redesigning their life.

You can see the despondency in their eyes. You can see the weariness draped over their tired frame like a badly hung curtain. And if you listen hard enough, you can just about hear the muffled cries of their unsung heart.

"It doesn't excite me to wake up in the morning"
"I don't know what I want any more"
"I wish my life was different to how it is"

Hiding behind our busyness with work, with being mum, with being wife, and with being the executor of a million other chores, will not make our unhappiness disappear, or make our silent dissatisfaction go away. Our frustrations will only scream louder as time passes. Eventually we will either explode, blaming everyone else and life itself for our predicament, or implode on ourselves with a nervous breakdown. Resentment will slowly poison our heart and body, and shrivel us up into a sour, juiceless woman.

We owe it to ourselves to stop and say enough is enough. Carrying on as we are will exhaust us and bleed us dry. Instead of focussing all your energies on a doing mode from dawn to dusk, make *you* count. How? By taking *me* time. Time for deep reflection, time to get into the stillness of your own heart. Turn your mind inward and become more conscious of your own thinking process. You are everything you have ever wanted. Start this amazing journey of self-discovery right away. Don't postpone your joy. You deserve it.

A JuicyWoman knows that she is first and foremost Woman before she is wife, before she is mother, or any other roles she plays. She realises that a happy woman means a happy lover, happy wife, happy mother and a happy friend. To help her get in touch with her deep self, she regularly peels away each role she plays in her own mind and meets what is left standing. Far from that being nothing, she comes to see the exquisite beauty of her own being and the unstoppable joy of her own loving heart.

There are three people in you:
The person you think you are,
the person other people think you are,
and
who you TRULY are.

12

You Are First and Foremost a Spiritual Being.

Whether you notice it or not, you are a spiritual being. You are the wisdom you seek, and the Love you hunger for. And you possess more power to change things for the better than you are presently aware of.

You don't have to follow a particular religion to access this unlimited spiritual might. Your spirituality is beyond religion. There is a vast difference between religion and spirituality. Religion is man-made, while spirituality exists as a fundamental part of what we are, regardless of what we do or don't do, or whether we are a 'good' or 'bad' person. These days, while some of us may find religion unappealing, we must be careful not to throw out the baby with the bathwater. To negate and ignore our spiritual side would be our greatest loss: the wondrousness of our human experience depends on it.

What is the spiritual in a woman? It is her absolute certainty that she was born good. She does not believe any of the rubbish that says she was born a sinner or somehow imperfect, or any of the thoughts telling her she is not good enough or has to strive harder to be a better person. She only has to wake up from the nightmare that is going on in her own head to see what a remarkable and godly creature she is; that her so-called imperfections are simply the mistaken creations of her confused mind.

The spiritual in a woman knows that there is a natural order in life, that there are no victims, only contracts between individual souls to serve for the awakening of the highest good. That what the physical eyes see as cruelty and atrocities are simply blessings in disguise, sent to tear open our own loving heart when we believe it should stay closed in the name of protection and safety. At the moment we seem to need war, calamities, abused victims and starvation as a means to discover how sweetly our heart loves. And when we awaken to our true glorious nature, we will stop perpetuating this illusion of a seemingly cruel life. Only then will we notice that heaven is already here. We don't have to go to any religious sect to do that. We only need to enquire.

A lot of our suffering comes because we are ignorant of how life works. We are determined to keep our upside-down view of life and trudge on, regardless of the times we falter and fall, without stopping to investigate and look for a sweeter way. We can be such stubborn creatures of habit, determined to hold on to beliefs that only serve to hurt because our mind is too afraid to believe we deserve only good.

Our view on life must encompass the spiritual dimension for us to live a truly fulfilled and blessed life. We must take our spiritual development seriously and make time for spiritual endeavours. If we have unresolved issues that are holding us back from functioning happily in the world, we should seek help, make peace, put them to rest and move on. You cannot change the past; it doesn't exist anymore. Once you free your mind and your emotions from being stuck in the dead zone of the past, you will have more energy available for the unearthing of your luminous spiritual self. Question: *Who am I? Why am I born? What is my greater purpose in life?* Meditate on them and let the answers surface from the depth of your being.

Focus on your personal and spiritual development. We live in blessed times – there are countless good books available on every spiritual topic you can think of, innumerable courses for us to learn from and enlightened teachers to guide us. Everything is available at our fingertips. There is no excuse for spiritual ignorance save laziness. Your own good self is standing by, waiting for your attention. Your Love-self is constantly blessing you but you may have been too busy to notice. Everything that's happening, is happening *for* you, not *to* you. It is all good. It is all for your benediction. When you truly know this, your divine excellence will blaze forth.

A JuicyWoman knows that the brilliance with which she shines in her life is entirely dependent on her commitment to developing her awareness and dedication to her spiritual nature. The quality of her life advances at the same rate as the momentum of her spiritual development. She uses everything in her life as fuel for this awakening of her delicious self. Whatever happens, she sees it as a blessing in disguise. Knowing this truth brings her the peace that surpasses all understanding.

❦ ❤ ❤ ❤ ❦

*Only Love is good enough
to fill my mind
and colour my world.*

*Only Love is boundless enough
to keep increasing
as I keep giving it away.*

*Only Love will exalt me.
I never knew this,
but Love is who I am.*

13

Love is What You Are

Love is your natural radiance. It is the juice of who you are; not something you have to earn or work hard to achieve, or be lucky to have bestowed upon you. Whether you believe it or not doesn't alter this truth. Love is radiance itself. That's why people glow when they are in love. You can't have one without the other because they *are* each other.

Love is the purpose for which you are born, and Love is who you are. In other words, the reason you are here is to be your very own self. Women are put on this planet to glow, to radiate their irresistible light. And the only reason why we are not glowing is because we believe the stories in our head; stories that say we are not good enough. When we stop believing the lies our mind tells us, the veil falls away and we get to see the astonishing light of who we are. Then we are in love with our self and the world, because we get to see that we are the world.

When we say Love, we don't mean the sentimental emotions you feel towards someone you're fond of. It is not the kind that has 'hate' as its opposite either. Neither is it the type that can start and then stop when you don't get your own way. The Love we are talking about here is the truth of *what* you are. It is your openness, and it includes everything, the so called good and bad. It's the open arms in the face of pain because it sees everything as itself. It is your naked brilliant self when you go beyond the stories you have about yourself in your head. Its miraculous light heals everything it touches.

Although we are born as this amazing Love (look into the eyes of a baby and it's obvious), the reality of it somehow deludes us. Who you truly are, and the person you believe and experience yourself to be, seem to be galaxies apart. This happens when we have spiritual amnesia. We forget our true face. Externalising it, Love becomes something to *have* rather than something to *be*. It is a strange chase we do, running after what has always been inside us all along. Love becomes something we try to own because we think we might lose it rather than something to give away because we are the endless source of it.

A JuicyWoman is a woman who sees life with different eyes. She is not conned by the world of apparent duality and conflicting opposites. She sees all as herself, as Love beckoning to Love, as Love joining with itself. She endeavours to see every conflict as an invitation to return to the Love she is. Rather than get caught up with the stories in her head, she questions them, and having met them with understanding, she stands as the clear light of unhindered Love again.

*Let my heart burst its banks
from knowing too much Love!*

14

Self-Love is a Healing Agent

The true extent of Love's power is still unbeknown to humankind. Modern life at the moment is polarised towards the material rather than the spiritual. Success is measured in terms of possessions and status rather than how happy and at peace one feels. The treadmill of material gain has kept us so occupied, mentally and emotionally, that we have no time to pursue and investigate the deeper, more spiritual aspects of ourselves. So even though this Love essence is who we are, by our own ignorance and lack of knowledge of its inherent nature, we deny ourselves the most powerful force in the universe.

As a general rule, we tend to reserve our love for those in our immediate circle, and especially the ones who agree with us. This love takes on an air of exclusivity. We also equate the word love with thoughts like *I love chocolates* or *I love sitting in a café enjoying a hot cup of coffee*. So, unknowingly, we deprive Love of its true power, artificially reduce its excellence, and normalise it as just another emotion, like sadness or anger.

A Japanese man was diagnosed, at the age of thirty, with terminal cancer in the lungs and kidney. He wasn't at peace with the fact that the radiation treatment and chemotherapy he was receiving was killing his healthy cells as well as the cancerous ones. So he discharged himself from hospital and decided to *love* his cancer instead. A radical move indeed. *"I created it,"* he said. *"It is part of me."* From that point on, he vowed to use all his energy to *love* the diseased part of him, rather than fight it. He completely changed his diet and lifestyle. Thirty years later, his presence now radiates joy like a beacon of light, and he sees every new dawn as the birth of a beautiful new day. To him, his cancer was the result of his non-loving attitude towards his body, and by changing the attitude back into one of Love, his new way of life put his body back into harmony with his spiritual self. That made him healthy again. He now spends his time inspiring others with this radical approach.

We are not implying that one does not need medical treatment when one is ill. Of course it is important we seek medical help when necessary. What is being highlighted here is the untapped power of Love. There are many more people who have stories like that of the Japanese man. If we take time to investigate, we would be amazed at how often these miraculous recoveries do take place.

Did you know that there is no door that Love will not open? No wall that Love will not bring down? Only Love can disarm fear. Love is the cohesive force that keeps the universe together. And Love is the unseen glue that literally holds your body together too. Families break up when Love leaves (usually through the backdoor, unnoticed), and our body too falls apart through lack of self-love.

Do you take time to listen to what your heart is saying? Do you stand by your decisions, and do what you feel is right and appropriate for you? Do you exercise and give your body the food and water that it needs to stay nourished and healthy? Do you take time to do the things you enjoy? Do you like the person you see in the mirror?

Or are you too afraid to stop and listen in case you don't like what you might hear? Do you go along with the rest to keep the peace even when it means going against your own grain? Do you try to avoid looking into the mirror for too long because you don't like the 'imperfections' you see? Are you far too busy to do the things you enjoy? Believe it or not, this is what a lack of self-love looks like.

When we fall ill, it's a message that our body is not at ease with what is going on in our life. This disharmony is simply a loving message telling us to pay attention to what is happening inside us. Numbing the pain out is not the answer. Returning to Love is. We do that by taking notice and not ignoring what is gong on inside us. We do that by making it a priority to sorting out any issues that are troubling us. We do that by taking good care of ourselves on the mind, body and spirit level. This is what kindness looks like. This is what self-love looks like.

*A JuicyWoman knows that her health is the barometer of her happiness —
happy woman = healthy body. If she is not experiencing good health, she
goes in and takes note of what is making her unhappy. She investigates her
thoughts, as healing first begins in the mind. Having put right her
thinking, she then makes the necessary changes. It might mean she takes
time out for herself. Or put her attention to sorting out some relationship
issues that are troubling her. Having attended to the root cause of her
unhappiness, her body is then free to heal.*

❧ ❤ ❤ ❤ ❧

*Your mind has no right to intrude
upon your inner silence
and rob you of your inner peace.*

❧ ❤ ❤ ❤ ❧

15

You Are Never Upset
For the Reason You Think

It's not easy to keep your cool when you feel you're being attacked. Our mind is quick to justify why the person has no right to upset us, and the feeling of injustice makes us want to lash out too. There are two fundamental facts worth knowing:

- You are never upset for the reason you think.
- You are upset because you see something that is not there.

You may think you're upset because the person has said an untruth about you. But if you know the truth about yourself, why would it upset you that he or she sees a different perspective? It's not possible for them to see you from your viewpoint. In fact, no one can. We always only see the other from our own point of view, because the only filter we have is in our own head! When we truly get this, we will stop needing approval from anyone else but our own self.

It is more likely that you are upset because you need that person's approval. You need them to validate who you think you are. You don't realise that the only person who can do that is you. No one else can do that for you. Perhaps you are upset because deep down you know you should be giving the approval to yourself.

Usually you are upset because you perceived the other person's actions as an attack on you. In truth, the attack is not there. It is more of a cry for help, because to seemingly hurt you, that person must be hurting inside. We hurt when we are not happy because joy is our natural state. You'll never find a happy person lashing out unkindly towards another. We do that when we are stressed and unhappy. It is our disguised scream for help.

A JuicyWoman knows that she is never upset for the reason she thinks. She will start by investigating her reaction to what has happened, because she understands that a grievance is self-inflicted. If she does not take it personally, then it cannot trouble her. She knows that life is always kinder than her mind tells her it is.

❧ ❤ ❤ ❤ ❧

A prayer is a winged thought
that brings Love
and Light
into a dark moment.

❧ ❤ ❤ ❤ ❧

16

The Power of Prayer

It's easy to doubt that prayer works because we have been conditioned to put our faith into what's tangible, and we are suspicious of what our five senses cannot pick up. We underestimate the power of prayer because our physical eyes cannot see the subtle changes that take place after the prayer has been made. Our lack of understanding of our own divine nature also prevents us from seeing the true extent of what a prayer can do. We find it hard to believe that 'little old me' can perform miracles. Perhaps this true story will help.

A woman was caught in a pile-up involving a few cars on the motorway. The shock of the accident was so great that it propelled her into an out-of-body experience. She found herself standing by the mangled heap of what was left of her car, looking at her crushed body behind the steering wheel. Suddenly, she was aware that she could literally hear people's thoughts as if they were speaking them aloud. As clear as day, she could hear one man feeling exasperated being held up by the traffic from the accident, thinking, *"Damn, this is just what I don't need right now!"* As she glanced around, she noticed a ball of light, luminous and bright, rising from about five cars down from where she was, moving towards her. In that instant, she knew somehow that someone from that car had sent her a prayer. Just before the ball of light hit her, she took a quick glance at the number plate, memorised it and, as this light entered her, she could feel herself being sucked back into her body. She woke up in hospital, and when she finally left after her serious injuries had healed, she traced the number plate with the vehicle licensing agency and turned up at the person's house with a huge bouquet of flowers!

Prayer is one of the most powerful spiritual tools that we have at our disposal. It is transference of healing energy to the one in need of help. And the miracle it brings is beyond what our limited mind is capable of imagining. This immensely powerful force is available for us to use at any time. The most powerful prayers are the ones that are made from the Love-centre of your being, with absolute conviction that prayer works. The moment we truly invoke God's presence (which is what Love is) into any situation, healing has to take place.

A JuicyWoman understands that pain and suffering are created by the mind when it has forgotten its own Love nature. The same is true for illness. Healing begins the moment the confused mind is aligned back to clarity and Love. A prayer is simply a winged thought that brings Love and light into a dark moment. Her lips are always ready to invoke a prayer whenever the need arises.

❧ ♥ ♥ ♥ ❧

I love myself.
Therefore I choose to have faith in the good,
invest every second of my life
in positive thoughts,
and doubt the negative ones.

I love myself.
Therefore I choose to let go of the past
and forgive myself and others
for all wrongs done to me,
and trust that everything has served my soul well.

I love myself.
Therefore I have no regrets,
realising that in each moment
I had always done the best I knew how,
and I am thankful for the wisdom I now have.

I love myself.
Therefore I am open to miracles every day,
knowing that miracles
are natural expressions of Love
and I am this Love itself.

❧ ♥ ♥ ♥ ❧

17

Unleash Your Luscious Radiance

Every moment that you love, you emanate luscious radiance. A woman who loves for the sake of Love itself is her true Juicy self. Like sweet pheromones to unguarded hearts, her beauty is both captivating and alluring. Both men and women alike will find her appealing and will want to be around her sweet aura. It's as if simply being with her causes their nerves to calm and their negativity to evaporate. Her presence somehow makes it easier for them to believe in what is real and good. Dreams of the heart seem more possible in her vicinity. This is because a woman who loves is a holy woman. And there isn't anything her holiness is not capable of.

Many women today have lost their way to this inner sacredness. Some barely manage to stay afloat, as exhaustion, comfort eating and deep loneliness threaten to suck them into annihilation. The harder they work, the further they seem to be from their happiness. The more they strive with cosmetic surgery and all the other kinds of treatment available to achieve 'better looks', the more dissatisfied they feel about their appearance. No wonder depression is on the increase. Those faring slightly better suffer from dissatisfied relationships, or no relationship at all.

The collective Woman is dying from not being seen in her beauty and glory. God made Woman an embodiment of his divine beauty. We are meant to shine effortlessly. And we do, when we are not stressed, riddled with guilt or filled with anxiety about the future. We do, when our heart is open and we feel carefree as opposed to being careful.

Every woman needs to be *seen*, whether she is aware of it or not. Just like a flower, a woman feels beautiful when there is someone there to behold her. But the first beholder of her beauty has to be her self. If she can't see her own beauty, the chances are no one else can either. Seeing one's own beauty has nothing to do with vanity. It's the way of self-love.

It is our way of acknowledging God's gift to us. False modesty doesn't make us feel beautiful. Gratitude and graciousness does.

You are radiant when you live not only with openness but *as* openness itself. Living as openness means you have no aversion to anything. You are so transparent and fluid, so confident and happy within yourself that you welcome all, just as it is. You are not threatened by anything on the outside so you are able to welcome life as it is and not how you think it should be. Instead of being preoccupied with the internal dialogue that argues with reality, you stay gracious and relaxed, knowing that everything in life serves your highest good. You don't give in to the constrictions of the personality because you know you are more than that.

You are radiant when you are unafraid. Being unafraid means you know that you are safe and secure no matter what. It means you don't join in with fear and discontentment when those around you are moaning and fretting about life. You can see that it is confusion in one's thinking that causes misery, not life itself.

You are radiant when you do not mind being a fool, for love, for all things honest and good. Innocence becomes your garment of light. Boldness is your natural sparkle. You remain relaxed in situations that people find stressful, challenging or awkward.

A JuicyWoman knows that her radiance is not something that plastic surgeons can carve out. She firmly believes fillers of any kind belong on DIY shelves and not in her. Her radiance comes from being at ease with herself and with life. She is a lover of what is, knowing that what is, is good. She knows there is no point or wisdom in resisting what is, because it doesn't work. Fighting what she has no control over only creates suffering. On the other hand, being a lover of what is allows her joy to be constant. This naturally causes her to exude radiance of the most attractive kind.

❧ ❤ ❤ ❤ ❧

The voice of my heart,
in the stillness of nothing,
she whispers to me.
"You are."
That was all she said.

❧ ❤ ❤ ❤ ❧

18

Your Heart is Your Compass

One of the hardest things for a woman is to do what is right for her when others don't agree with her choice. We think it's because we don't want to upset the people who disagree with us. But it is actually our need for approval and acceptance that makes us hesitate or compromise when our heart is telling us something. We are also afraid that if we don't do what others want, we might not get what we want from them. This often unconscious manipulation creates a vicious cycle. The more we listen to their preference, the less we honour our own voice; the less we honour our own voice, the more unsure we become; the more unsure we are, the easier it is to override the intuitive voice of our heart and follow the crowd, even when they are heading in the opposite direction to where we want to go. We are caught in a no-win situation that leads us further away from our truth.

It is vital to our sanity that we use our heart, and not our head or someone else's opinions, to show us the way to our happiness. But we also need to tread with caution here and learn to tell the difference between the voice of the heart and the voice of emotion. As females, we usually live in our emotional centre, and that makes this distinction doubly tricky. What we think is coming from our heart could well be a knee-jerk reaction from our emotions when we're not pleased with the way things are. So how do you tell the difference?

- There is an inner calm when your heart speaks.
- It comes from a loving place inside you rather than a defensive one.
- You have an inner conviction that, no matter what, you have to follow and stand by it, even if it doesn't turn out the way you think.
- You are at peace no matter what the outcome.

It's not common practise to listen to the voice of our own heart. It takes courage to follow the heart. It takes boldness to step out of what we think is expected of us and do what we feel makes us happy. It takes clarity to ignore the voice of guilt that's rambling on in our head, telling us not to be selfish. But Love is totally selfish because it wants to give itself to itself. Once it is realised that true giving can only come from what one *is* rather than what one pretends to be, it's not an option not to be the person you are. Until you are authentic, there is no real giving. Anything else will only bring resentment and heartache. If your thinking doesn't stand in the way, your heart, as the compass of your soul, will point you towards all that's wonderful and good.

A JuicyWoman knows that if she doesn't live her authentic life, no one else will. She also knows that to hear her heart, she needs to make time to be quiet inside, away from people, phone or distractions. To be her own best friend, she needs to listen to herself. Then, whatever happens, she can stand by her self with no need to blame anything or anyone. Living from an honest place, she is at peace.

*When your life gets to a point
when it's just between you and God,
that's when miracles
become a daily occurrence.*

19

Woman + God = Goddess

A true goddess is a woman who lives from her inner domain of spirit. Rather than using the outside to make her the person she thinks she ought to be, she lives life from the inside, radiating outwards the gift of who she is. She knows that her core, the centre of who she is, is deeply spiritual.

This core draws its power and strength from a source that far excels the limited knowledge of her thinking mind. 'God', 'Spirit', 'Divine Intelligence', 'Universe', whatever the terminology, it is the matrix of the unseen, and her understanding of it extends beyond the parameters of religion itself. The name is of no consequence to her. Instead of taking on someone else's idea and concept about God, she takes time to decipher God for herself. Bit by bit, layer by layer she de-codes this all-pervading energy. She gets right to the root of her spirituality, this field of pure intelligent and self-knowing consciousness that has no trace of fear in it. She comes to know that she can never be separated from this source; that any separation that exists is only in her own mind. She also knows that the same applies to every human being, whether they know it or not. She also knows that another name for this source is Love.

When a woman has awakened to her own Love nature, the power to heal all misunderstanding, the clarity to see beyond all conflicts and the freedom to always be in joy become her birthright. Regardless of what takes place on the outside, she feels deeply loved and supported by life. To her, God is synonymous with Love, Love is synonymous with life, and life is what is. Resisting nothing, living becomes a sacred artform to her. Her unified vision sees all as useful and good.

A JuicyWoman is a goddess because she knows that life is a spiritual journey. Every experience, be it positive or negative, serves as a blessing to awaken her to her divine nature. She constantly seeks to give her highest gift to whoever crosses her path. She lives her life fearlessly and to the full.

We tune a musical instrument
before we use it
to make sure its notes are precise.

We align the mind
through meditation
to make sure it creates the reality we want.

20

Increasing Your Juiciness

One of the ways we stay connected and centred in our all-pervading goodness is meditation. Meditation is now a common tool that people use to de-stress, improve their health and concentrate better. Artists, writers and designers use it to increase their levels of creativity. Athletes use it to enhance their performance, as a calm, focused mind has a direct strengthening effect on the body. Business people use it to relax their busy minds and tense bodies. The benefits that meditation brings are countless.

There is also a higher purpose to regular meditation practice, and the payback for this is considerable. This will make sense when we open our mind to the invisible realms. First, there is a higher as well as a lower nature in us. The lower nature is our superficial self and is preoccupied with worldly matters and survival issues. It has short-term interests. Fear is its trademark. Our higher nature, however, works with a different paradigm. It is our Love-self and is aware of the bigger picture. It has implicit trust in goodness, and immovable faith in the divine. Love is its motivator. Meditation or stillness permits us to access this higher nature, our wisdom.

Meditation allows us to go beyond the static noise of worldly confusion to the inner silence where answers lay waiting. The practice of sitting in stillness provides a chance for the mud of fear to settle and for clarity to reveal itself in the face of whatever uncertainty we have. Through training, the mind is eventually silenced enough to enter into the all-knowing stillness. For those who have their faith in God, *'Be still and know I am God'* become words of great significance. It is said that when we pray, we talk to God, but when we meditate, our mind is stilled and God speaks to us. This inner voice becomes the direct guide to each and every move we make, and we will never be far away from deep peace, happiness and fulfilment of the soul. Taking the time to meditate is like putting your plug into the heavenly socket, which leaves us spiritually energised and strengthened. Reality for us will be effortless and sweet when we are not running around like a worn-out battery.

Stillness in meditation is the key that unlocks this inner treasure house. Vibrant health, abundance, sublime peace, loving relationships, beauty, grace, miracles, joy, wisdom and freedom are neatly stacked on these golden shelves, waiting patiently to be claimed. Everything is generously available when we unlock this inner door. The door to this inner vault can only be opened by the stillness of our being. In silence, we will discover that we are an energy field of pure potentiality. Contained within us is a matrix of infinite possibilities. We can be as successful, as joyous and as abundant as we desire. All we need to do is:

- To believe it is possible
- To focus our intent and attention on it.

We use our thoughts to manifest what we want from this field of pure potentiality. This is how the unmanifest becomes manifest. We are indeed architects of our own destiny.

A JuicyWoman knows she is not functioning at her full wondrous capacity as a spiritual being without taking time out to recharge. Meditation is food for her soul. Through stillness, she gets to go beyond the stories in her head to see how sweet reality actually is. Her benevolence becomes obvious to her uncluttered mind.

Everything you are
you have manifested
from the universe
of your own mind.

21

Your Intrinsic Greatness

The woman in you has untold strength and power to create. If only you could glimpse for a brief moment the magnitude of your womanly being, you would be blown away by how breath-taking you are. And when you come to know this amazing self, all the tension you hold in your body in trying to be someone 'better' will dissolve away in a flash. You will stand free, mentally unencumbered, wide open and grateful, loving every moment that life brings to you.

This beyond-the-thinking-mind self is ever-present with inexhaustible energy and resource, ruling your destiny each and every moment. This 'she' dwells deep in you and can reach into the highest level of wisdom to give you the answers you need.

Most women are unaware of this aspect of themselves. We are more familiar with the *'I'm only human, therefore I'm not perfect'* self. This self preoccupies itself with resisting reality/what is, and trying to control what cannot be controlled. These two activities keep us firmly engaged full-time, and many sweet and wonderful things go unnoticed! With so many ongoing stories in our head, the drama of living seems all-consuming.

The awesome fact that we are this wondrous, deep-knowing being is difficult for us to really take on board. Our mind is more comfortable believing in our frailties and imperfections rather than our excellence. When faced with challenges, instead of being fired up, ready to show what we're made of, we doubt our capabilities and strength instead. By doubting, we undermine our chance to grow and to fulfil our full potential. After years of habitual doubting, we end up dimming our great effulgent light into a faint glow. We lose the ability to believe that we can achieve whatever we desire. We unconsciously opt to hide inside the protective shell of our comfort zone.

Self-attack is one of the main ways in which we compromise our greatness. We are quick to criticise ourselves for being not good enough. *What's the matter with me? I can't seem to get things right! — I hate my bum. It's too big!* We keep inflicting these unkind thoughts on ourselves. How are we supposed to feel like a woman in command of her own glory if we keep running ourselves down without a second thought? We become champions at covering up our lustre with a veneer of low self-esteem.

Self-doubt is another form of self-attack. *Who am I to think that I can achieve my heart-dreams? Who am I to think I have gifts to offer to life? Who am I to imagine that my light can show another the way when they stumble and fall?* In our own mind, we have shrunk ourselves so small that mediocrity is a safe bet for us. We find it hard to entertain that we have wondrous gifts to offer to life. Not only do we doubt what we can give to life but, tragically, we also doubt what we can give to our self. We doubt our ability to know what is right for us and to trust that inner voice. We doubt the intuitive voice that warns us when something is not right; we carry on without caution and end up having to clean up the mess. We ask for advice when we already know the answer.

- Self-doubt undermines your power to create success in all areas.
- Self-doubt causes you to settle for less than your heart's desire.
- Self-doubt weakens the healing potency of your loving heart.
- Self-doubt veils you from the awareness of your JuicyWoman.

What can you do when self-doubt plagues you? Question the thought itself. Ask: *Who is the authority behind this voice in my head? Why should I believe it without question? Can I know for sure what it's saying is true?* And, more importantly, *Why should I make my decisions based on what it says?* Set the doubt back on itself – **doubt the doubt!** The voice of self-doubt is not your true voice. It's your conditioned mind that believes in fear and limitation. Your true voice is always kind, loving and supportive; anything else is just a lie that throws your mind into confusion.

Guilt is yet another form of self-attack. There is nothing virtuous about guilt. And neither do we get extra brownie points. We have made the mistake of thinking that feeling guilty means we care. We feel guilty putting our feet up when we're tired because we feel things need to be done. We feel guilty that we're enjoying ourselves if others are feeling miserable because we think it's insensitive. We feel guilty taking time out to replenish our soul and spirit because we think everyone else's needs should come before ours. We think that's what being a good woman is about. Wrong. When we enquire deeper, we see clearly that a happy woman also means a happy partner or wife, a happy mother, a happy daughter, a happy friend and a happy colleague. Your relationship with yourself is the determining factor for all the other relationships in your life. Any discord you feel about yourself ripples out to every single relationship you have with others. So, far from attacking yourself with guilt whenever you do something to appease your own soul, see it as self-honouring. Remember, the happier you are, the more useful you are to humanity.

Every thought that says we should be different from the person we are, is a form of self-attack. It makes us feel that we are not good enough. Such thoughts create stress and constantly put our psyche under strain. Our neuro-psycho system then works overtime to artificially inflate our self-esteem by criticising others to compensate for this inner sense of inadequacy. We end up being defensive and guarded, as well as being critical. This attitude sours and hardens our soft beauty. This acidic, fault-finding behaviour corrodes the soft feminine allure that is naturally there when the heart is open and kind. In other words, being critical makes us ugly. It strips us of our natural God-given purpose of being Woman: to inspire life with our beauty and grace.

When we attack ourselves with our own thinking, we automatically project this thinking outwards and assume others are attacking us too. The subliminal belief that the world is out to get us contaminates our thinking patterns. This kind of thinking makes us see the world out there as unsafe. How do we turn this around? Cease the hostile thinking in your own mind and the world out there will look different to you.

A JuicyWoman knows that life itself is benevolent and unkindness can only be born from a confused mind. Being benign, she refrains from any form of self-attack, be it self-doubt or guilt. And when she does not harm herself or others with her thinking, heaven starts to reveal itself in her own front room.

You will come to realise
what you are
when you have seen through
and let go
of what you are not.

22

Identification with Things Causes Spiritual Amnesia

For many, the world we live in is filled with pleasurable and attractive things. From our lovely house and all the nice objects that we find space for, to the gorgeous clothes we stuff into our wardrobes and the matching shoes and handbags that we take delight in collecting, we love them all. While masculine energy is all about going forth and achieving goals, our soft feminine energy is about opening wide, drawing in and receiving. We are luscious women and our feminine energy loves us to be filled, if not by love, then by food or material things. Hence men will never understand how we can still fall in love with another pair of shoes and feel the need to acquire them while we already have thirty pairs waiting in our wardrobe! Unless we have the makings of a Zen nun, most of us will continue to delight in gathering more beautiful things into our already fully laden life. We simply love being filled.

There is nothing wrong with having lovely things, and lots of them for that matter. There is nothing un-spiritual about that. The material things in themselves are neutral and are neither good nor bad. What we need to watch out for is our reliance on them to raise our social standing or to make us feel more acceptable. The age of consumerism persuades us that we need to be seen with the right brands if we are to be 'somebody' in society. So we use external things to project an identity that we think will increase our 'somebody-ness', be it with our *Jimmy Choo* heels or *Vivienne Westwood* outfit. The kind of things that we identify with will vary from woman to woman, depending on our age, social class, financial situation, the kind of people we mix with, the latest fashion trends, and so on.

The truth is we are not actually attached to the item itself. It's the projected value we put on it that makes it so attractive. You might think that if you wear what is in at the moment, it means you're a fashionable woman. Perhaps a pair of *Manolo Blahniks* will increase your kudos with your girlfriends, especially if they are fashion-conscious. Or if you have nice cars parked in your drive, maybe your neighbours might think more highly of you. We use objects and external things as a form of self-enhancement, as a statement of who we are.

The retail therapy mentality is just that: trying to find who we are through things. It doesn't work. It only drives us to keep looking for more, to keep buying, to keep consuming. We end up with wardrobes, shelves and every available space stuffed full of things, and still we look for more. We have far more than we need, and still we have this intense desire to acquire more. Momentarily delighted with a new purchase, it doesn't take us long before we move onto the next thing. Somehow having more doesn't satisfy us, or make us happy in the long term.

We will never feel the deep contentment of being filled and satiated through acquiring more things because what we're looking for cannot be bought. What we're looking for is our self-worth, dignity and self-respect. What we're looking for is intense joy and freedom. In fact, what we're looking for is... our very own self! And nothing in the material world can give us that.

A deep awareness of your spiritual nature and a conscious connection with it will end this crazy chase. It is an internal investigation rather than an external buy. *What is the meaning of my life? Why was I born? What are my deepest gifts in life? How does my outlook affect my life?* These questions will lead you into the depth of who you are. You are the one you have been waiting for. And only you can give you what you need. Nothing else can do that for you. Anything else blinds you from your own shining and brilliance.

Identification with things causes spiritual amnesia. Observe your relationship with things, especially those that have 'my' attached to them. Do certain things make you feel slightly more significant and superior? Does not having them make you feel inferior to those who have more than you? Awareness of how you have misguidedly associated your own value with these external things will free you to appreciate how wonderful you are just being you. You will never know this true self in the depth of your being until you have mentally stripped away the need to use external things to prove who you are. This does not mean we need to get rid of our possessions. Possessions in themselves do not do anything. It is only our relationship to them that needs to be redefined. We can have everything and still be free.

A JuicyWoman enjoys every single lovely thing that comes her way, be it a gorgeous frock or a sparkling pair of heels. But she knows her loveliness is beyond all things physical. Undistracted by external things, her connection to herself remains deep and honest, allowing her authentic self to shine through in each moment.

❧ ❤ ❤ ❤ ❧

You love me. Good.
You don't love me. Good.
When I can be happy,
regardless of whether you love me or not,
then I am free.

Only when I am free
do I know how to be truly happy,
and I become a gift to you
because I am the kind happiness that stays,
no matter what.

❧ ❤ ❤ ❤ ❧

23

To Be Happy, We Need to Be Close to Happy People

It seems that pure, unadulterated happiness has become more and more elusive in our daily life. We may have advanced in technology, but the same cannot be said for our state of happiness. On the contrary, it seems the more possessions we have, the more we think we need and the less satisfied we are. Having more money at our disposal may mean more pleasures, but it's not the same as being happy. Being happy means we are relaxed, deeply contented, and serenely peaceful. This modest goal has become the most difficult to achieve.

These days we are all too willing to lower the bar on the scale of happiness. When a woman says she is happy, it means she is coping. It means her material security is not being threatened, mouths are being fed and bills are being paid. It means she is 'satisfied' that everything in her life is ticking along and there's no major catastrophe. *I'm ok and the people close to me are fine too, so I've no complaints.* Such is her level of happiness.

We have forgotten what it means to be ecstatically happy — when your heart is humming with constant joy and your body electrified with life-force. Your mind is free because it doesn't believe in fear, and your soul is at the forefront of your life, manifesting your life purpose. Your face glows, your body flows and your heart is generous.

Now how many individuals do you know who fit this description? Not many. Such people are a minority indeed. Instead, we have depression on the rise and doctors prescribing anti-depressants left, right and centre. Emotionally we feel fragile, and we are easily offended. We stop believing we can have it all. There is a quiet desperation as we continue to trot on this path of mediocrity, feeling neither vibrantly bright nor brilliantly happy.

What is going on? How can we turn this around so happiness becomes part of our everyday reality? One of the vital components for happiness is the ability to get on with people around you. In a nutshell, relationships. To be truly happy, you need to get on well with your partner or spouse, family members, friends and colleagues at work. This is because happiness comes from having happy relationships. Because of our inherent need to feel good, people who have given up seeking happiness in relationships resort to seeking pleasure without relationships: alcohol, drugs, casual sex, even violence. Pleasure that comes from sensation-gratifying activities often removes the need to interact with other people. This sort of pleasure gives you a short-term buzz, whereas happiness gives you a long-term glow. And until we create a society in which more people are happy, it will be impossible to reduce these destructive choices being made by so many of us.

It's in our genes that we need people in our life. And to be happy, we need to be close to happy people. The more happy people we have around us, the greater our chance for happiness. It also works the other way round — the happier we are, the happier people around us will be. This is because happiness is infectious.

To get on well with people, we need to lower our guard. Instead of being defensive, be open. The world is full of goodness, and blessings come to us when we are open. See only good and you will attract the same. Everything in life happens not *to* you but *for* you. They come bearing gifts, so be ready to welcome all with open arms.

Being open with people also involves a willingness to be vulnerable. It means revealing our tender side. It means exposing our soft underbelly, which actually makes us more feminine.

Being open also means to have no agenda. When you are open with a person, you don't impose anything on him or her. You don't need others to have the same views. Even when they disagree with your ideas, you don't feel threatened. An open attitude is an open door — wonderful interactions can flow back and forth, nurturing both your gentle hearts.

We are also more available for good relationships if we don't take offence easily. When someone seems to be having a go at us, the automatic reaction may be to feel offended. It could be the tone of their voice or the look on their face. We feel hurt and closure happens. Slam! We shut them out of our heart. In truth, the seeming attack may not have anything to do with us. Deep down they are unhappy, and their behaviour towards us is simply a cry for help. See beyond the appearance of their action. Of course, we must never stand for any kind of abuse from anyone. What we are referring to here are those times when we fall out with family or friends because of what they said about us. It's never about us anyway; it's about the person's perception of who they think we are. It's not possible for anyone to truly understand us. The quicker we let go of the need to be understood, the happier we will be. The more you know who you are, the less affected you will be by what others think of you. And when you are not easily offended, you are a better friend. Your heart remains open and spacious, allowing you to be compassionate. Only Love begets Love.

Forgive, forgive, forgive. To forgive means you are willing to free yourself from the trauma and misery of the seemingly unloving act inflicted by the offender. To forgive doesn't mean you condone the act. You forgive because you love life more than you love suffering. It is insane not to forgive, because what has been done cannot be undone. How does bearing a grudge in your heart help you to live a brighter life? It doesn't. What helps is adopting the attitude: *I forgive because he knows no better.* Resentment will only eat away at your peace and devour any passion left in your soul. If you could see how precious you are, you would give yourself this release.

Every single person in your life has gifts for you. Some gifts are obvious, like love, the joy of sharing, warmth, support and laughter, while other gifts are not so evident. Nevertheless, they are there if we know how to identify them. The gift an angry person brings could be for you to practise patience. Or if you don't like the look of somebody, it's usually because there is a part of you that you have yet to embrace in yourself. The gift in this case is for you to open your mind, to investigate your thinking and gain a better understanding of yourself. The world is like a mirror in which we can see our own reflection. Any aspect that we feel an aversion to is the very part of us that is calling us to love. And the day we can love ourselves unconditionally, we will be a lover of all life.

A JuicyWoman knows that every single person in her life is God-sent. Each comes bearing gifts of untold value for her growth and self-realisation. She knows that an enemy is a good friend in disguise. Her eyes see beyond appearance, while her heart listens to the other's heart. Only seeing kindness and benevolence, her reality is always a gentle one.

꒰ ❤ ❤ ❤ ꒱

I am happy
not just because things are going well for me,
or that I live in a nice house
and have lovely holidays.

I am happy
because I know how to distill joy
from ordinary moments
and see everything as a gift.

24

Happiness is a Choice We Make

Most of us think we need a reason to be happy. When we have this belief, we make happiness conditional without meaning to do so. It means we require things to be a certain way before we allow ourselves to feel light-hearted and joyous. Why limit our capacity to be happy? Why restrict the opportunities for our heart to feel uplifted? A sweet life lies in our ability to be happy for no apparent reason. We are happy because happiness is our natural state. And our natural state emerges when we no longer believe everything the mind says.

Happiness is not a given grace. *It is a choice you make.* Each now-moment is an empty space that you choose to fill with a particular emotion or state. If you spend the moment criticising or complaining, it means you've filled the empty moment with negative energy, a downward force that suppresses your natural, carefree state. And misery is what you'll get. But if you choose to notice that in your life you are being given so much, without any effort on your part, gratitude will spread its wings and descend on your grateful heart. Take a moment to consider that the ground always supports you wherever you may be. That your heart beats perfectly without any volition on your part. And that the earth is always offering you a vast array of colours, sounds and scents to delight your senses. All you have to do is notice.

Each instant is an un-made moment. It is a blank screen, ready and available for you to decide what you want to experience. With free will and the power of choice, we choose how this moment turns out. Focus on a fear and you're filled with stress. Focus on appreciating what you have and the moment is sweet. If you so choose, your now-moment can be filled with inner peace and great tranquillity. Your heart can sing with joy because you realise that the power to be happy is nestling in your very own loving palms.

The term 'happy-go-lucky' is not just a saying, but a formula. Basically, the happier you are, the luckier you'll get. This is because a happy person radiates light, and light is always attractive. The light that emanates from a happy state draws goodness towards it. This is the law of attraction. Imagine for a moment that you are lady luck herself. Would you move towards someone with a smiling disposition, or someone who looks glum and miserable? We will always gravitate towards a person with a sunny outlook. Every living thing, be it man, woman, child or animal, would naturally be drawn towards a happy individual rather than a fed-up one. The same goes with goodness — it will always lean towards a person with a happy temperament. A happy person is more attractive and magnetic in nature. She naturally attracts goodness because the vibration of happiness is in accordance with it. In other words, happiness and luck vibrate and resonate at the same frequency. The happier you are, the luckier you will be. So if you want to be lucky, BE HAPPY.

A JuicyWoman is a woman who realises that happiness is as available as the next breath. All she needs to do is to make the 'happy choice'. She does that by focusing her attention on what is right, rather than what is wrong. She redeems her power to make each moment as delightful as she wants by letting go of the need for there to be a reason before she can be happy.

When my heart sings
the delirious joy of Yes,
and my soul dances
the spell-binding rhythm of Yes,
I know I've finally arrived
- in myself.

25

The 'YES' Mantra

Yes is one of the most powerful words in the human language. It has a life-enhancing quality and we are literally strengthened when we affirm *Yes*! and mean it. *Yes* gives the vibe of an open door, of possibilities, of allowing potential to be fully discovered. A positive, hearty *Yes* can instantly flood our veins with life-force, and when chanted repeatedly with a positive mental picture in mind, it can be an effective booster when we are feeling low. It can be more effective than drugs, and there are no nasty side-effects either! As scientists move further into the quantum field, more and more evidence will be uncovered about the life-affirming properties of *Yes*.

Since *Yes* has such empowering qualities, it would be smart of us to make sure we have a *Yes* mantra repeatedly in our heart and frequently upon our juicy lips. Rather than gossip about the woman next door, chant *Yes* instead. It doesn't matter whether we do it silently or out loud. Even without focusing the mind on any particular content, after just five minutes of chanting *Yes*, you will feel invigorated and energised, ready for life. Your body will feel tingly and warm; life-force, also known as *prana* in yoga terms or *chi* in tai chi terms, gushes through your bloodstream, renewing your cells and regenerating your organs.

Observe yourself. Which word do you say more often in your everyday life — *yes* or *no*? To help yourself, find more opportunities to say *Yes*. It could be for little things as well as major decisions. Would you like a drink? *"Yes, not now, but I'll have one later"*, rather than *"No"* because you're not thirsty right now. *Shall I move into the countryside like I've always dreamed of doing? "Yes"*, rather than *"No"*, or *"I'm not sure because it might not work out"*. It is the *Yes* attitude that will carry us into new dimensions and new frontiers. It is the *Yes* outlook that will stretch us far beyond our edges of fear to discover the fresh and exciting potential that still lies dormant in our being.

Take the *Yes* test and find out what percentage of your life you have managed to bring to sweet fruition. Answer the following questions, count the number of times you say *Yes*, and check out your score below.

1. Do you feel happy ninety-nine percent of your waking hours? ....

2. Do you totally love the person you are? ....

3. Do you feel vibrant and healthy most of the time? ....

4. Do you love waking up in the morning, filled with enthusiasm? ....

5. Do you adore the job you do? ....

6. Are you in a job that nourishes your creativity and spirit? ....

7. Do you have good women friends that inspire you? ....

8. Do you have good men friends who make you feel sweet and feminine when you are in their company? ....

9. Does the thought of family bring you a sweet sense of joy, warmth and support? ....

10. Are you in an intimate relationship that feeds and nurtures your feminine heart? ....

11. Do you feel totally at peace with your past? ....

12. Do you feel relaxed about your future, knowing that all will be well no matter what happens? ....

13. Do you feel happy and content in your own company? ....

14. Do you love silence and stillness as much as you love
    activity and merriment?   ....

15. Is your spiritual self in the driving seat of your life,
    manifesting every heart-dream and sweet longing
    you have?   ....

16. Do you genuinely believe that nothing is impossible for you? ....

17. Are you aware of your soul-purpose, and are you
    fulfilling it?   ....

18. Do you feel love and a deep connection with all life?   ....

19. Do you care about other people's happiness as much as
    you care about your own?   ....

20. Do you have a conscious day-to-day living relationship
    with your spiritual source?   ....

You get five points for every 'Yes' you have put down. You get zero points
for a 'No' and the same goes for half-hearted answers like 'Sometimes',
'Sort Of', 'A Little Bit' or 'Maybe'. The total score will indicate what
percentage of your potential you have manifested in your life so far. The
more your spiritual self runs your show, the more of your potential you
will be able to fulfil. The more of your potential you maximise, the easier
and more effortless the joy of living becomes for you.

*Emotional intelligence is JuicyWoman's forte, so you can be certain that
the Yes mantra is never far from her consciousness. Harnessing the power
of Yes whenever possible, vibrant aliveness is one of her many shining
qualities. She is always ready for the next adventure or inner discovery.
Her prayer is to live life open and to the fullest of her beating heart.*

᙭ ❤ ❤ ❤ ᙭

Suffering has nothing to do
with the world.
It has to do
with your thinking.

When you start to question
your thinking,
you will see that
the cruel world you once thought existed
is actually a beautiful Love-filled paradise.

᙭ ❤ ❤ ❤ ᙭

26

The Nature of the Undisciplined Mind

We take it for granted that what goes on in our head is there with our permission. We identify with each random thought that appears, and presume that we are the 'I' in the thought. We assume what the mind churns up is valid and reliable.

When you investigate this 'thinkingness' more deeply, you will soon see that it is an endless procession of opinions and commentary about anything and everything. It also constantly reprocesses old information, going over and over again what has already taken place, five minutes before or decades ago. It also relentlessly evaluates and passes judgement on things, events and people that don't even concern us. So who is the perpetrator behind this crazy mentalisation?

The *superficial self* is the culprit, the aspect of the mind that has assumed an identity that believes it is separate from the symbiotic nature of the whole. This superficial self is completely invented by your mind. It is who you *think* you are, rather than who you *really* are. Mind has invented this imaginary identity out of self-preservation and fear. It is the voice in your head that says you can be easily hurt by others, so you need to be on the defensive, just in case. It is also the voice that says you should worry about your future because you never know what's around the corner. It is easy to spot the superficial self because it uses fear as a legitimate way of living, rather than Love.

Your superficial self usually argues for your limitations rather than encouraging you to step beyond your comfort zone. It does not cheer you on to explore the million and one potentials you have inside you. It is the voice that persuades you to play safe rather than be bold and adventurous. It is the one that has you believe you are weak and incapable. It is the one that proclaims *"I can't"*, rather than *"I can"*.

We have identified with this superficial self for so long that we don't realise the mutterings in our head aren't ours and are not worth the attention we give them. Each time a thought comes into our head, we presume we are the thinker. So we engage in its content, giving value and importance to it. We can even have an entire monologue with an imaginary audience in our head!

We see the thoughts as significant and important because we think they are 'my thoughts'. These thoughts are egocentric by nature, hardly surprising because they are the offspring of the ego, another name for the superficial self. Take the constant barrage of opinions our mind seems to form about one thing or another. In truth, opinions have no intrinsic value. You may feel more important because you have a view about something, but only because you believe having a view validates you. You don't need to have opinions to be validated. You simply are, regardless of what you think or what others think. In fact, the more we relax into who we are rather than striving to be something else, the happier we are.

Until you consciously take up the role as the central command of your mind, it will hold you captive and make you suffer with its whims and confused thoughts. Mind is only useful when you give it a job to do. Tell it to focus on a particular task, and constantly train your awareness to question and transcend the random thoughts. Otherwise, watch how it intrudes upon your silence and inner peace!

Undisciplined thinking costs you more than you know. This unremitting mental activity burns up a lot of your energy and time. This means you have less at your disposal for more useful or joyous experiences. Many a sweet moment is missed because of this internal, mindless chatter. When your mind is preoccupied with the rubbish thoughts, you also miss out on the clarity a clear, calm mind gives you. With this clarity, you feel more spacious, less cluttered, more relaxed and less anxious about your life. Anxiety is promoted by a mind that does not understand how life works, and so is afraid. When there is true understanding, no anxiety can ever invade your inner peace.

A JuicyWoman will not take her thoughts for granted. She meets each one with kindness and enquiry. In doing so, she is free from the tyranny of an undisciplined mind. She is aware that her mind is a double-edged sword, a powerful instrument that needs to be handled with care. You will find her keen to learn the art of meditation because she knows the quality of her life depends on it.

❧ ❤ ❤ ❤ ❧

I am not my thinking.
I am the truth behind my thinking.

❧ ❤ ❤ ❤ ❧

27

Only Your Thoughts Can Cause You Pain

Everything you see represents your thinking. If you believe there is such a thing as injustice, you will see a world where 'good' people get hurt and 'bad' people get away with murder. You will not see that the universe is a fair and good place. *"But that's what happens in life!*, you may exclaim. Not so, if you truly understand how life works.

It is common knowledge that you reap the seeds you sow. In other words, what goes around comes around. Life is an efficient bookkeeper; we are accountable for every thought, deed and action, and so is everyone else. Whether they know this or not, it does not affect the precision with which life counter-balances each act. As an observer, we do not have the ability to truly know the full picture. What is seen as unfair is only because something is being judged purely from the point of view of how it appears. Things make more sense when we look at a situation from a spiritual perspective or soul viewpoint, because we are not just finite human beings. This means seeing the bigger picture, rather than just a specific detail at a particular point in time. When we understand the law of balance or *karma*, the law of cause and effect, we will see that it is not possible to escape from the consequences of our actions, be they kind or otherwise. At some point or another, we will feast upon the fruits of our own planting.

It is your thoughts alone that can cause you pain, and your thoughts are far more unkind to you than reality actually is. If someone speaks to you in a harsh way, it has more to do with the other person than with you. To take it as an attack or a personal insult only leads to more conflict and unhappiness. By having such thoughts, you cause pain to your own sweet heart. Perhaps the other person is struggling with some personal issues? Instead of retaliating or withdrawing from the person, we can extend our loving attention to them. *"I can see you are upset about something. If it's something I have done, then I'm genuinely sorry. Is there anything I can do to help?"* Such an approach will neutralise any negativity that is there and nip any unpleasantness in the bud. Most of all, it will bring peace back into your heart. A peaceful heart is always a happy heart, and a happy heart is a healthy heart. Your wellbeing springs from a daily practice of responding in a peaceful and loving way towards all life.

No one but your own self can affect you. There is nothing in the world that has the power to make you ill or sad, weak or frail, if you do not allow it to do so. You are your own authority. It is you who have the power to influence all things by recognising your spiritual nature.

We have also been programmed to expect pain. We even have a saying, *'No pain, no gain'*. This is actually saying pain is good for us! How crazy is that? So we wander around with our radar subconsciously homing in on pain because we want the gain it gives. By believing in this seemingly innocent saying, we are drawing pain into our life without realising it. Right now, delete the word 'pain' and replace it with 'joy' – *No JOY, no gain.* By consciously choosing joy as a way to grow, joy is what your soul will attract.

When pain is seen in its true light, it actually disappears. When you perceive emotional pain, it means you are looking at the situation with confusion. You are confused because you believe it is possible to be a victim. You hurt yourself by thinking that. Healing begins the moment you take responsibility for your own joy.

A JuicyWoman knows that to exit the world of pain, she only needs to lay down her own hostile thinking. The refusal to see the 'bad' in others also releases her from self-judgement and guilt. What makes her gorgeous is her benevolence and the generosity of her loving spirit to forgive and forget. To her, that is a sane way to live. Anything else is unnecessary madness.

‰ ❤ ❤ ❤ ‰

The quality of your life
depends not
on what you have
in your life,
but
what thoughts you have
in your head.

‰ ❤ ❤ ❤ ‰

28

The Power of Awareness

Have you noticed that there are certain scenarios in your life that you can recall almost detail for detail, or conversations word for word, without any effort? You remember the tone of his voice, the flutter of your charmed heart, the warm night air like a soft blanket against your skin, and the sweet sound of his voice as you snuggled close to him, transported into a haven of tenderness and delicious warmth? Well, you can remember every facet of this shining diamond of a moment because at that moment you were not busy in your head, lost in 'thinkingness'. The brilliance of that instant is still in your mind because you were completely present when it took place.

When we are present, when we give the moment one hundred percent of our attention, our awareness captures every bit of joy and magic that lies waiting around every corner. We find pleasure in the most ordinary of things. We are available to observe the thousand and one delights that nature constantly displays for us. Enchantment and glee are our everyday experiences because we are relaxed and quiet enough to notice the charm in ordinary moments.

But when we are preoccupied with the incessant chatter in our head, everything seems mundane and dull. Every time we listen to the random ramblings of our undisciplined mind, it is like jamming each available frequency with discordant screeching, so that you never get to hear beautiful melodies and heavenly music! How awful is that? Yet, unwittingly, we allow this mental madness to pervade our consciousness every single day.

So how do we create more of this silent respite in our mind so that we are totally available to be thrilled and enthralled by the thousands of blessed moments that march through our life every single day? It is time to come out of the narcissistic closet of our untrained mind and enter into this glorious garden of enchantment. Yes, contrary to what religion says, we have never left the Garden of Eden.

Notice how unkind the mind can be, how consistent it is in putting you down, how quickly it condemns your not-so-perfect move in different situations? Notice how mean and unnecessary it is when it comes to criticising people? A mind unregulated by our awareness is a tyrant.

If you want to increase your joy and happiness, then you must train your mind.

Training the mind is no easy task. It's like taming a wild horse. But with diligence and a commitment to succeed, it will gradually come to heel and become a useful ally. The first step is to discredit the mind for the random thoughts it produces. In the beginning, you may find that you are reluctant to let go of a random thought because you perceive it as useful. Questioning each thought and seeing it for what it is, rather than engaging in its story, will help you let go of your attachment towards it. Without the preoccupation of haphazard thoughts, your mind is clear and your awareness shines through. You will find that without effort, and too much planning, you will know exactly what needs to be done and when. You will move and respond with ease and without stress, to every situation that arises. You will know the right words to say at the right time. Remember those golden moments when the most profound words flowed from your lips and you wondered where they came from? Well, they were from your very own juicy awareness. Rather than perceiving, believing or even hoping, awareness *knows* just what the moment requires and delivers it.

Learn how to be more *present*, rather than *mentally absent*. To stay present to the moment is a conscious choice because the mind has this uncontrolled tendency to wander off. Left to its own devices, the mind flips in and out, be it during an encounter with a person or with nature. This flipping in and out of awareness means we never get to dive deep enough to really enjoy the present moment.

Being present is to say, "Let me be here in the now to receive each blessing that life gives me." To be present means to trust the good in every moment. To be present involves a willingness to be opened, to receive gracefully. Less thinkingness means more awareness. More awareness means less unnecessary, hurtful thoughts. Less hurtful thoughts means more joy and more inner peace.

A JuicyWoman is keen to master her mind because she knows it can be a tyrant. To tame it, she practises devaluing its mindless chatter. Meditation is one of her spiritual tools. She knows that without these conscious efforts, the mind drifts off into egocentric thoughts, making life seem mundane and problematic. With a quiet mind, her awareness can find delight in anything and everything.

ও ❤ ❤ ❤ ও

You don't know who you are
because you have never gone beyond
the stories in your head
of who you think you are.

ও ❤ ❤ ❤ ও

29

The World is a Mirror in Which You See Your Self

It is common for us to look out at the world and not like what we see. We mistakenly think that the picture we are looking at has nothing to do with us. What we don't realise is what we see on the outside is merely a reflection of our internal dynamics and beliefs. We are only capable of seeing what is part of our own internal mental blueprint – this is the law of seeing.

"People hate me" stems from one's own inner hatred.

"The world is full of untrustworthy and suspicious characters" is a symptom of mistrust within you. You probably have difficulty trusting your own sense of judgement.

"People are very sweet and kind" mirrors your innocence and light, and a willingness to help others.

"I see good in everything, even adversity" shows your alchemical ability to transform negative situations into positive ones.

Your world without is simply a mirror of your world within. If you have a pessimistic nature, you will tend to have a negative take on things. This takes away the benevolence from what you see; your view will tend to be a dark one rather than one that is bright and cheerful.

Your inner world is the *cause*, and your outer experience the *effect*. To change the effect, you must attend to the cause. Your inner world is a subjective world that consists of a whole matrix of thought patterns. We know them as beliefs. Every thought is a cause that manifests an effect. This is obvious when you consider how a thought can change the way you feel in a split second. For this reason, it is absolutely essential that you manage your thoughts so as to bring forth only desirable conditions for yourself.

Most people try to change the effects by working with the effects. This is futile as you are only swapping one form of distress for another. To remove the seeming affliction, you must remove the cause, and this cause can only be found within. Understanding this relationship between your inner world and your perceived outer reality will show you where your spiritual work needs to begin — with yourself. When you have a good understanding of this immutable law, you will no longer be troubled by outer circumstances. You will hurry back into your inner domain and align whatever thoughts or beliefs you have with joy and peace.

We need this mirror because it is difficult for us to see ourselves objectively. Living in our own skin and looking out of our eyes, the 'I' that we believe we are is often too caught up with its make-believe identity to be able to see our internal patterns clearly. This is why having the world as a mirror is useful. If you don't see a beautiful world, then seek to find that beauty within. Then look up again, and you will notice the loveliness in an ordinary rock, a rainbow or even a dull and gloomy day. If you tend to notice war and violence, then look inside and see where it is that you are at war with yourself or with others. We need to realise that guilt and criticism are themselves a form of violence.

A Juicy Woman is wise enough to know that she needs mirrors to see what she is and what she is not. Never disheartened by the fact that she has human flaws, she welcomes all reflections. She uses the feedback from outside to take the appropriate action and reconnect with her spiritual self. She sees it as an invitation back to the loving-kindness of who she is.

What you discover
is a product of your intention.
In other words, what you find
depends on what you are looking for.

If your intent is malice,
war and conflict is what you will find.
If your intent is kindness,
only the sweet and the holy will be yours.

And if your intent is always
for the highest,
Love's perfection is what
your blessed eyes will eventually see.

30

How to Obtain Your Heart's Desires

Every woman holds precious dreams in her heart. Most of us subconsciously conclude that if we're lucky, we might get our dreams, and if we're not, there's nothing we can do about it. Often we simply let these deeply buried and unspoken dreams fade away into nothingness. We may not be silently yearning anymore, but on the inside we are quietly despairing. We may think that whether we get our dream or not is down to some random intervention by an unseen hand. Nothing could be further away from the truth.

Our future is *totally* within our field of influence. It is not at the mercy of any whimsical or unpredictable external power. Power to shape our reality comes from within because we are part of this universal mind called God. All we have to do is to pay attention, to understand how these divine principles work, to harness these dream-supportive energies as God intended us to do, and to bring forth all that our heart desires. It is God's will that we are happy because when we are happy we are a blessing, and we instantly become useful to life.

The recipe for success is very simply this:

Intention + Attention = Certainty of Success

What is intention? It is the purpose or goal behind your action. It is the psychic plan that motivates you to act. It is the driving force behind what you do. Your intention determines whether the fruit of your labour will be bitter or sweet. The nature of your intent also affects the potency of your plan of action. The higher or more spiritual the intent, the more power it has to attract what you desire, because it is in accordance with spiritual laws. Low intent means *my aim is to get what I want regardless of how it affects others*. A high intent not only has the objective of achieving what you want, but also serves or gives to others at the same time. If the intent is of a spiritual nature, you have a whole legion of invisible powers ready to help you. It is like floating downstream in a river: the current carries you along with very little effort on your part. So making our intention a spiritual one actually causes the universe to conspire with us in our endeavour.

For example, say you want to be with the right man. If your motive is to be with a man because you are needy and want someone to love you and take care of you, the chances are that men will stay away, or you will attract the 'wrong' type — someone who is as needy as you are. But if your motive is to be with a man because your heart is full and you want to give your love, you will have no trouble attracting a good one. This works because it is in accordance with the law of giving that says: *We must first give in order to receive.* So whatever you do, make sure your intention is of a spiritual nature. It will then seem effortless to achieve what you want because your goal will have the natural power of the universe behind it.

Once you have a clear idea about your motivating force, and it is a kind and loving one, you need to apply the attention to the matter in hand. Attention is your mental focus — what you concentrate your energies on and where you place your awareness. What we pay attention to, we energise. What we energise, we bring to life. So if your goal is to be with the right man, you need to pay attention to your thought patterns and behaviour as you pursue your goal. What are your beliefs about men? Do they tend to be positive or negative? Do you have negative expectations about intimate relationships? Are you needy and emotionally demanding when in intimate relationships? All these, if they go unresolved, will hamper your chances of recognising the right man. You need to be aware of your internal patterns when it comes to intimate relationships. Being conscious of your patterns and actions means your subconscious, negative behaviour cannot sabotage your goal unknowingly. Instead of your neurosis driving you, you have a clear say in how you want to act and behave.

Another aspect of the 'attention' is to hold the vision of your goal in your mind at all times. You think of the idea, you dream of it, you live on it. Most of all, you need to believe you can have it. It is not uncommon for women to say they want to have a beautiful, intimate relationship, but don't believe they can have it. What you can't visualise, you can't claim. What you can't claim, you cannot have. You need to be able to see, in your mind's eye, you in a sweet and beautiful relationship with your beloved.

The next part of this powerful formula for success is the need for consistent effort, which is part of the aspect of attention. This is what separates the lightweights from the heavyweights. The ability to put in consistent effort, directing your energy and time into doing what needs to be done in order to achieve your goal, is the mark of one who succeeds. The lightweights will give up after a few half-hearted attempts and wonder why they fail. Living in a quick-fix and gratify-me-now society has made us less patient, less steadfast and less enduring in the way we work towards achieving whatever makes us happy. We try something for two minutes, then give up and say it doesn't work!

Our always-in-a-hurry, always-too-busy culture has given us an unrealistic expectation of quick results, and if that doesn't happen, we move on to the next thing. Gone are the days when one had to do seven years of apprenticeship before one could be regarded as a master in one's craft. These days we have people who undergo a weekend of training and call themselves 'masters'. Unfortunately, in such situations there is simply not enough time for training to make sure the practitioner of the therapy has the discipline and integrity to develop the required skills.

So in order to achieve our heart's desires, we must be constant in our effort. Giving up too quickly is very often the only reason why we don't achieve what we want. Our heart and mind must be unwavering when it comes to putting in the time and energy required.

Let's get back to the example of attracting the right man and keeping him. First, let your intent for the relationship be the joy of loving him. Visualise yourself in a beautiful relationship. Then be vigilant in spotting any sabotaging patterns you have, especially in the dating stage.

And forget about pointing out his patterns, they are none of your business. They are his responsibility, not yours. Practise self-honesty and face up to your own negative behaviour and neediness. Have the tenacity and commitment to work through all of it. Once you have sorted out the negative patterns in your psyche, you become so irresistible, radiant and bright that your beloved has no option but be drawn straight to you!

Success is certain. The universe is benign. You are a child of the universe. It wants you to have what you want. It wants you to be happy. You only need to know how to operate in harmony with its immutable laws. Hence, the more altruistic your vision or goal, the more support you will have from the universe to manifest it.

A JuicyWoman knows about the unseen power of intent. She is a weaver woman who weaves every single one of her dreams into reality by the divine mixture of right intention, right attention and right action. She knows that when a goal is held clearly in thought, with consistent effort and attention, its manifestation into physical reality is only a matter of time. And she, above all else, is a friend of time.

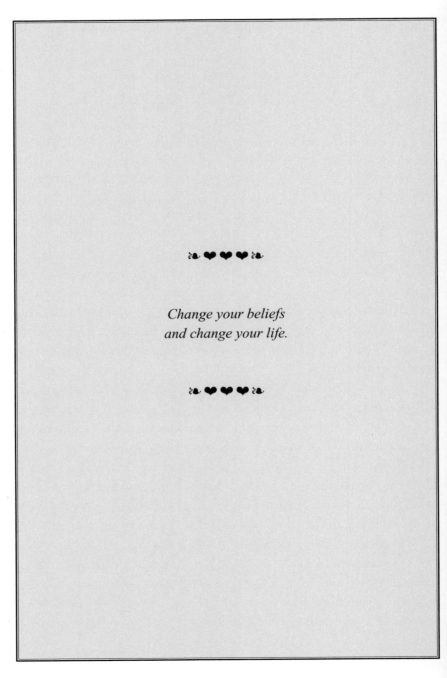

*Change your beliefs
and change your life.*

31

You Can't Change Your Genes, But You Can Change Your Beliefs

It is not your genes that determine what kind of life you have – it's your BELIEFS. Your beliefs are the foundation of your personality. They define you as worthy or worthless, powerful or powerless, self-reliant or dependent, and so on. Your beliefs have far reaching consequences, both positive and negative in your life. They also determine what you experience in life.

Examples:

If you have a belief that in general people are compassionate and caring, then you will experience help appearing whenever you need it, even in the most unpredictable hour, in the strangest of places. But if you believe the opposite is true, when you're in difficulties, no one seems to be about. And even if there were people around, you may deem them unsuitable to help you.

If you believe that you are worthy and lovable just as you are, you will experience being loved without having to make any effort at all. If you believe otherwise, then whatever you do is never good enough and you will feel unvalued and unappreciated for the person you are.

What you see is simply an *effect* of your belief. It's like wearing sunglasses – you will see everything with a tinted effect. Likewise, your beliefs make you look at life in a certain way. It's also true to say that most of us don't see things as they really are. What we see is usually an inaccurate interpretation based on our own belief system.

It seems that we can't alter the DNA package we inherit from our parents, that we have to settle with our lot, whether we like it or not. The good news is that there are now stunning new scientific discoveries that show that it is not our DNA that control our life and determine the way we are, but it's thoughts that affect the cells in our body that results in the way we are. Epigenetics confirm that a cell's life is controlled by the physical and energetic environment and not by its genes. This exciting find means we must take a good look at the physical environment we live in, the emotional environment that we women often swim in, and most of all, the mental environment that we perpetuate in our own mind in the form of thoughts. Your beliefs are patterned thoughts, the templates from which the design of your life is stencilled. So if you want to change your life, this is where you need to focus your attention.

So the first piece of good news is that we are not victims of heredity. The next piece of fabulous news is that you can *reprogramme* your beliefs. Just like the software in your computer, you can delete old ones that don't serve your happiness and install new ones that do. Cancer may run in the family, but if you get rid of cancer-provoking thoughts, which in turn curbs cancer-engendering behaviours and instead, have a healthy and happy attitude towards life, who knows – you could be spared. Worth having a good try, don't you think?

We may not be able to change our DNA but we can definitely change our beliefs, whatever they may be. There are techniques out there to reprogramme our beliefs, from positive affirmations to various other mind-induced methods. There is also PSYCH-K, a technique using kinesiology and whole-brain postures to integrate new positive beliefs into the subconscious mind. What is clear here is that if we want our life to change, we cannot take a disempowered attitude, sit back, do nothing and expect things to be different – *If you always do what you've always done, you will always get what you've always got!"* We need to re-wire our brain which in turn affects our body's cellular structures if we want to maximise our joy and freedom.

You won't find a JuicyWoman lament at being given a poor lot from her parents. Whether they are 'good' parents or 'bad' parents, she is grateful to them for giving her the gift of life, a tremendous gift in itself. If she doesn't like the look of any aspect in her life, she turns to the subconscious in her mind and re-write the software in there. To create new possibilities, she is aware that she needs to be vigilant with regards to her thinking patterns. Consistent effort and right thinking are the names of the game to change her beliefs, thus changing her life.

❧ ❤ ❤ ❤ ❧

God loves you.
You are precious to him.
Forgive and forget
whatever has happened
and begin to make your life
something beautiful for God.

❧ ❤ ❤ ❤ ❧

32

Feeling Sorry For Yourself Holds You Back

NEVER NEVER NEVER do the *poor me*. A poor me mindset instantly strips you of your personal power. You feel victimised, at the mercy of the seeming perpetrator or situation which makes you see the world as an unfair place. When you do that, you also subconsciously see God as unjust and uncaring. This distorted way of seeing undermines our faith in goodness and subtly makes us turn away from our own divinity.

Refuse to see yourself as a victim in any situation. Resist the temptation to succumb to a mindset that finds emotional sympathy an attractive option. We're drawn towards such a mindset because of its payback. One of the paybacks of being a victim is that someone else and not you, is responsible for the mess. This way we don't have to take any personal responsibility towards what has happened. Unfortunately as we deny our responsibility, we also deny our power to make the situation better. Doing so also puts us at the mercy of others to decide how we should feel – in heaven or in hell. Now what sane woman would want to do that?

The other payback for being a poor me is the 'sympathy food' we relish when our friends exclaim, *"Oh you poor thing! Fancy having to go through all that." "I don't know how you cope with that. I would have gone to pieces!" "Oh, how awful. That should never have happened to you."* Our superficial self/ego laps up every drop like sweet milk to a thirsty cat as if all this sympathy is good for us. Let's wise up here. Do you ever walk away afterwards feeling empowered and good in yourself? No you don't. Emotionally, this 'sympathy food' may temporarily sweeten our grievance but it doesn't make us feel strong and able. It's more like we are left feeling hard done by, a pawn in an inconsiderate and merciless world.

Another unconscious appeal of being a victim or poor me is it allows me to justify why my life is not wonderful or fantastic. *"I had these awful things happen to me. That's why I am the way I am now." "I can't help it that my life's a drudgery – it's no fault of mine that I had such an appalling upbringing!"*

We must shift ourselves out of this victim mode if we ever find that we have given in to its insidious charm. The cost of being a victim is high because

- we forgo our own authority to determine how we want to feel
- we forfeit our inherent power to make things better
- we disconnect from our spiritual self and stop being Juicy
- we disown our intrinsic divine nature and lose our radiance

We all understand that sometimes we may want to wallow in self-pity a little. But while we lick our wounds in the corner, the luscious woman in us is being sabotaged. In that moment we need to check and re-check, if being a *poor me* with a bedraggled aura is really what we want. Otherwise, take responsibility for your own happiness, and be the radiant resplendent goddess that you truly are.

A JuicyWoman endeavours not to feel sorry for herself if she can help it. And what helps her not to fall into that murky realm of self-denigration is her trust that everything that happens has a blessing in it. A willingness to be open and humility to be honest with herself helps her see the gift that lies waiting when her mind is clear.

Everything in the universe is precise.
There are no mistakes.
Everything that happens is a blessing.
There are no exceptions.

33

Intensify Your Spiritual Life to Have More Joy and Less Suffering

Suffering is *not* a requirement. Neither is it a necessity. There is no written rule that says to be human, we must suffer. The truth behind our suffering is ignorance – of how life's principles work. On our part, ignorance is a big letdown because it means we have inadvertently chosen to *ignore* this invisible matrix that governs all life. The lack of understanding (usually because we do not see it as a priority to pursue this spiritual knowledge) means we do unwittingly have pitfalls and we keep crashing into the same obstacles because we lack the astute awareness to identify them.

We also suffer when we drag our spiritual feet, and when our superficial self insists on having her own way. We give in to lower emotions and act upon them; in turn, they cause us more suffering. The sooner we apply our spiritual intelligence to sort out which way is fighting against the current and which way is being carried effortlessly into the sweet divine bosom of life, the better. The quicker it will be for our life to be more delicious and rewarding.

Spirit is the only real substance in life. Just as the sap is the true life of the tree, your spiritual nature is the true cause of your *natural* existence. What is natural is always harmonious and easy. By natural, we mean the way Love intends it to be – full of goodness and blessedness. It is only when we go against the natural essence of life that we encounter problems and hardship.

For example: when we have relationship issues, if we take a spiritual outlook, we would gear our actions towards neutralising the conflict by forgiving him and accepting that he is being the best he knows how at the moment. Rather than being self-righteous about our own viewpoints, we let go of the need to be right or to agree with each other. This will improve the peace we feel inside and allow harmony to prevail for us. Even if the other person refuses to make amends, we will still be released from the heartaches because we are no longer attached to the conflict. We no longer need the situation to be different from how it is. Live and let live is an intelligent approach.

Living from our higher nature is a powerful way to live. Our higher nature draws unlimited strength and immense power from the spiritual plane, the plane where Love resides. Everything we ever need can only be met and truly satisfied from this place. While our superficial self uses fear and separation as defensive strategies for survival, our spiritual self uses the unifying principles of Love to bridge every chasm our unenlightened mind throws at us. Emotional turmoil may cloud our judgement and sometimes we're not sure of the best way to respond. During such moments, if we were to ask *"what would Love do in this moment?"* the true solution would immediately be obvious. The insight would always be of a higher nature. This is a fabulous technique to help you see how your spiritual self would respond to the situation. If your desire is to be 'right', to have your own way, then this will not work. But if your desire is to be your finest self, asking the question *"what would Love do in this moment?"* will silent all supercilious thinking and point you to the summit of your radiant being. The fog of negative thinking will not stand a chance in the penetrating light of your holy self.

To intensify one's spiritual life is to live each moment with as much spiritual awareness as possible. Sure, we may falter at times, our knees may buckle with the seeming weight of injustice but the heart to be *who we can be* must ride strong. It takes a Juicy woman to do what's the best for the situation rather than what her emotions may dictate. Spiritual attitude when consistently applied will result in more joy and less suffering.

- Have absolute faith in the spiritual for all your needs.
- Forgive and let go of all grievances; they block the natural flow of Love.
- See everything that happens as an opportunity to grow, to develop your spiritual muscles and awareness.

- Without exception, practice being kind to everything and everyone, including your own self.
- Adopt an attitude of service towards all life.
- Have a daily spiritual practice: meditation, prayer, spiritual studies. Each second you invest in it will bring you closer to your Juicy excellence.

A JuicyWoman starts her day by cleansing her mind and heart from within. It is a daily routine of casting out all prejudices, thoughts of sickness, fear and pain. She aligns her mind with Love's Mind and attempts to make her life a living prayer by intention, humility and surrender. As she rises, she directs her thoughts to strength, love and a strong desire to bless. She makes a conscious effort to be in alliance with all that is holy and divine. Her strongest desire is to be the true woman she is, her quiet presence nurturing all life.

Your Juicy Beauty

When a woman is living
from her spiritual core
she is totally irresistible
and her beauty
fills the hearts of men and women alike.

34

Mirror, Mirror on the Wall

Woman is the quintessence of beauty itself. She is here on earth to radiate the soft, loving exquisiteness that only a woman can. Sadly, most women think that unless they have model looks, they cannot attest to this heavenly bestowal. We don't have any idea about this divine gorgeousness that is imminently waiting to burst forth, like starbursts of magnificent magnolias at the herald of spring. In our desperate quest to attain a perfect body and flawless face, in our obsession to get our physical form right, we forget about the natural and effortless inner attributes that are extremely effective in highlighting our radiance and beauty.

In our youth-obsessed culture, we are constantly being bombarded from all sides with messages about how a beautiful woman should look. There's so much pressure to look good that we have now resorted to cutting and carving our flesh in order to fit into this heartless paradigm. We voluntarily sentence ourselves to a torturous reality, where we are elated one minute and then depressed the next when the positive results start to fade away or become less obvious. We are back on the operating table, enduring unimaginable pain and discomfort because our sanity seems to depend on it.

Take a moment right now and inwardly reach out to every woman on this planet. Feel the turmoil and anxiety our collective laden heart is feeling in this cruel quest for physical perfection. Extend your tenderness towards each woman, for the pain she endures in the name of beauty. At the same time, let's gently ask ourselves: besides being injected with poison, being cut and hacked into shape and having bits of ourselves being sucked out, are there other more kindly alternatives that we can pursue in order to look good?

A JuicyWoman realises that there is an irresistible type of beauty that comes from the depth of her spiritual soul. She will first source her loveliness from this holy place before she takes more extreme measures, if she ever decides to take them at all.

Can you imagine
the kind of beauty
that not only charms the eye
but also captivates the heart?

35

The True Source of Your Beauty

There are some women to whom plastic surgery has given a new lease of excitement and confidence. And then there are others who took the risk, paid the money, endured the pain and still ended up with disastrous results – breasts that no longer stay where you want them, lips that look like inflated cushions, and skin so overstretched that it makes you worry that your face might split open if you dared to smile. No words can describe the inconsolable anguish a woman feels when her plastic surgery has gone horrifically wrong.

These physical manipulations aimed at enhancing our looks cost more than just our hard-earned cash. For many, whatever the improvement may be, it still leaves them plagued with stress and anxiety about the next thing they think needs fixing. We can't keep up with our dissatisfaction. Permanent contentment seems an unattainable goal. The beauty industry, with all its seductive methods, can be such a cruel world if we fall into its tenacious grip. At times it seems to give us what we want, but only momentarily. We can look into the mirror the following month and see new flaws and imperfections glaring back at us, stripping us of our self-confidence and feel-good factor once more.

It pains us to feel unattractive, or even unnoticed. Deep down, a woman yearns to look gorgeous and to feel that the world is her oyster, and she the shimmering voluptuous pearl, nestling comfortably within the luxurious fold of Love. There is something sweet and honest about this yearning. We have this need for attractiveness because beauty is one of our natural gifts as feminine women. We have an inkling that we've been put here to do a holy task – to be the embodiment of divine beauty, because beauty inspires. A beautiful woman finds doors open for her easily because beauty *enchants* too. And true beauty, a beauty that comes from beyond our moisturised skin, actually *opens hearts*.

Can you imagine the kind of beauty that not only charms the eye but also captivates the heart? And even when she is long out of sight, the fragrance of her grace still lingers on? This kind of beauty can only spring from a deep source. And the good news is that this kind of beauty doesn't stipulate that the woman be a particular size, have 'perfect' features, or be a particular age group either. This kind of beauty may not grace magazine covers, but it captures attention. It has a certain mysterious quality of grace and a loveliness that can be best described as radiance.

This radiance can only be sourced from within; there are no two ways about it. We can focus all our efforts on manipulating our outer form, but without this something extra that comes from our spirit, the look we achieve will be one of veneer, a covering over rather than a true radiance that shines brightly from a happy heart. A happy heart is a heart that is fed, not by the external, but nourished by the spring of your spirituality — Love. It's the depth of who you are.

Not everybody can be physically beautiful. Even those of us who are good-looking in our younger years may become crinkly and saggy in our older years. This process of aging is completely natural and kind, and we don't need to be so terrified of it. Age does not diminish a radiance that springs from our spiritual core. When you are so relaxed, so happy, so loving and so wise, no matter the condition of your outer form, you glow. When you are at peace and feel abundantly blessed, no matter how little or how much you have, you shine brighter than any star. It is the deep knowing that we are more than just flesh and bones, that life has a beautiful purpose, that makes us become truly beautiful. And it is when we know that Love is our nature, rather than something to acquire, that we become a woman of resplendent radiance. Our body flows with graceful ease. The light of spirit literally pours out of us. Everyone would want to have a piece of us to take home. Being unloved or unnoticed will never be part of our reality.

A JuicyWoman knows that it's not just her physical appearance but her disposition that enchants. She shines because she extends her interests beyond her own four walls, to the four corners of the earth and beyond. The glow of her beauty has to do with opening her heart to include every soul on this planet. It is her compassion that transforms her form into an art of grace. She knows that even the most beautiful will wrinkle and grow old. However, the beauty of a loving and generous heart will always shine with a rare light.

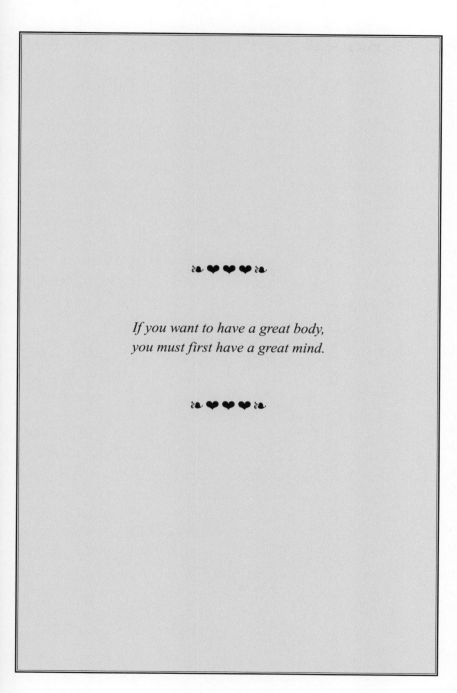

*If you want to have a great body,
you must first have a great mind.*

36

You Age According to Your Beliefs

Imagine a sixty-five-year-old woman crossing the street. Notice the clothes she is wearing. Observe the way she walks. Is there a light spring in her step, or does her body look tired and hunched over? Now zoom in to her face. Does she look a young and vital sixty-five, or does she look well past her glory? When you do this, you are seeing what you *believe* a sixty-five-year-old should look like. The picture in your head is based on the belief you have stored in your subconscious about aging. And you would not be far wrong to surmise that that's how you will look when you are sixty-five yourself. *You age according to your beliefs.* Quantum biology has now come up with evidence that every cell in your body is affected by your thoughts.

All the new sciences are pointing towards this: that we, as a thinking machine, as *consciousness*, have a direct impact on how we look, on how we feel, and on how our life pans out. Every thought counts in determining if you are going to end up a young, elegant sixty-five or a past-her-sell-by-date sixty-five!

Surely how one ages depends on other factors, you might argue, like if one is exercising, eating well, and making sure one's body and mind are constantly in a good state. Precisely! Every positive activity you do for your body has to come from a positive thought first. It is what you think that impulses you to act. And a belief is only a habitual thought pattern. There is no doubt that you can tell the quality of a person's thoughts by the state of their physical form and demeanour.

Another piece of shocking news is that we unknowingly accelerate the aging process in our body all the time. We constantly age our body much quicker than it needs to age. How? By having unconscious expectations about aging. If you pay attention, you can hear them muttering away in your brain.

"My knees are creaking, old age I suppose."
"My back is not so good these days, must be getting old!"
"No way am I going to sprint with you. I'm too old for that!"

The more you fear the aging process, the quicker you will age. The more you think you are not looking forward to being old, the faster you will show signs of aging. So most women are unknowingly hastening the very outcome they do not desire.

Why has the aging process provoked so much paranoia in modern women? Why do we have such a programmed aversion to this natural progression of life? Perhaps a lot of it is due to the fact that we equate our worth as a woman with how we look. Deep in our subconscious, we believe that looking youthful will get us what we want, that it will give us a better life. This type of thinking may indeed have a point because as women, we do take note that doors open easier when good looks are involved. There is no question that beauty does charm. But we need to get to grips with the reality that there is more to our beauty than just youth. Otherwise, Old Father Time, a pal you can rely on never being late, will drag us by the hair as we kick and scream all the way to our old age. Fighting aging with anti-aging behaviour or products is not the real answer. Anything we resist will only persist harder. It's a lost battle before we even begin. Why choose a no-win situation? That would be lunacy.

We are afraid to grow old because we lack vision and understanding about aging. When we put our self-worth into the youth basket, we will end up believing that when the tide of time sweeps us through the current of life, we will end up in stagnant pools, with flotsam and jetsam as chums. Such erroneous thinking is putting our sanity at risk. We need to question our thinking. We need to weed out these toxic beliefs.

Loveliness does not come from youth alone. True loveliness comes from knowing who you are. There is nothing more beautiful than a woman who feels completely relaxed and happy in her own skin, because she loves the person she is. Such a woman has no compulsion to screw up her beautiful body. Such a woman has no anxiety to distort the serene exquisiteness that naturally exudes from a happy face.

A JuicyWoman knows that her glowing worth as a gorgeous woman cannot be hindered by age — it can only be hindered by ignorance. She also knows that there is a kind of beauty that can only come with age, an irresistible loveliness that has wisdom scrupulously mixed in with it. This kind of beauty radiates a grace that only maturity can bring. And this can only come when she has a positive and loving attitude towards growing old.

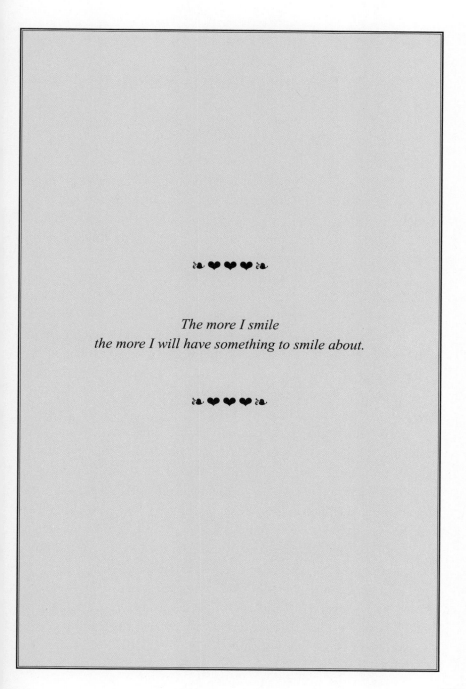

❧ ❤ ❤ ❤ ☙

The more I smile
the more I will have something to smile about.

❧ ❤ ❤ ❤ ☙

37

To Be Gorgeous, Keep Smiling

If we truly knew what a smile actually does for us, we would practically be smiling all day long! We wouldn't want to stop smiling because we would want to receive all the benefits a smile brings.

A smile that is genuine releases endorphins in your brain and makes you feel happy. You might think that you need something to feel happy about before you can smile. Well, how about smiling for the fact that you are alive, that you are breathing, and that you can enjoy a rainbow for the simple reason that you can see?

Did you know that flowers bloom and birds sing for your benediction? That such beauty exists because of you? You might think that thinking this way is arrogant. Actually, the reverse is true. When we become aware of how blessed we are, we become truly humble. In our humility, we begin to see that many things are given to us without any effort on our part. We begin to appreciate how the sun rises through no exertion of ours. We begin to love the ingenuity of life and feel grateful and exalted at the same time.

A genuine smile also brings energy into your body. The more you smile, the more energised you will be. Isn't that wonderful? If you wake up tired, try smiling a lot for the rest of the day. Make an effort even if it doesn't feel easy to smile in the beginning. Think of all the good things in your life and smile at each one. You will soon notice the difference. You will feel lighter because smiles are like wings, they lift you and help you soar higher into lovelier dimensions than the low, dark pit of doom and gloom to which the superficial self seems to be addicted.

Did you know that it takes a lot less muscles to smile than to frown? The saying *'smile and the whole world smiles with you'* is truer than we think. Like begets like, that's the law of attraction. If you smile at people, the odd one or two might not smile back, but most will. Research has found that people respond in kind to the facial expressions they encounter

— a smile for a smile, a frown for a frown. And if you want to bring out the best in someone, a genuine smile will tease it out rather than the opposite. A genuine smile is a gift, not only to the one you're smiling at, but also to yourself.

Some women believe that if they smile too much, it gives them wrinkles! This is an unfounded fallacy. The truth is that smiling actually lifts up the face and brings light to it. We instantly look more attractive when we smile. It is as if an inner light turns on and the face lights up. That's why lighting is crucial in a photo-shoot — to make models look brighter and more striking. A smile is definitely an instant beauty aid.

A smile also has an enchantment that disarms potential hostility. Providing it is not a sarcastic or sardonic smile, a smile that is genuine and warm can neutralise tension and dissipate negativity in a situation. Smiling and being happy is a good protection to ward off unnecessary 'downers' in one's life.

A JuicyWoman smiles at herself, smiles at others and also smiles for no good reason. Nobody needs to do anything to earn her smile; the mere fact they are alive is good enough for her. She does not need an external cause to make her smile. She knows that if she smiles first, what follows will be pleasant.

❦ ❤ ❤ ❤ ❦

It is your daily relationship with your body
that determines how attractive it is.

❦ ❤ ❤ ❤ ❦

38

Be Aware, Your Body is Listening

It is not uncommon for some of us to look after our pets better than we do our own body. The dog gets the right food, daily walks, supplements to ensure a shiny coat of fur, and lots of affection and cuddles too. But when it comes to how we treat our own body, the differences are considerable. We consistently chuck in any old junk, drive it heartlessly by not giving it the rest it needs, even when it screams exhaustion at us, and then rub salt into its wounds by criticising it for all the faults and flaws we think it has. Survey upon survey shows that most women are unhappy with their body, and for many this feeling even borders on hate. This is a rather strange way to show our gratitude for the indispensible gifts our body brings.

Do you realise your body is constantly listening to the messages you are sending it through your actions? Putting rubbish food into your body is a crystal clear message that you don't care about its wellbeing. If someone continually sends you messages that he doesn't care about you, would you still flourish and blossom? Would you glow and shine and feel beautiful? Of course not! Yet we think a consistent diet of unhealthy food is an okay message to send to our body. You wouldn't put a whole mix of petrol, washing-up water, diesel and bath water into your car and still expect it to work. Yet we put so much unwholesome stuff into our body and still expect it to carry on regardless. And then we have the audacity to be surprised when our body breaks down with illness or disease.

Caring means listening to your body's needs and giving it what it requires. Resting when the body is tired is essential. To say *"I'm exhausted but I can't stop because there is so much that needs doing"* is an example of the slavery attitude we inflict on our body. We wait until the body collapses from the strain before we stop driving it. We build up our tiredness until something drastic happens and we are forced to stop. Such unloving messages to our body are common, and it does not respond well to such an uncaring attitude.

You get from your body what you put in, not just in terms of food and rest, but also love. Your emotions shape your body. A woman in Love looks more radiant, her form lighter, and she becomes more graceful. So bombarding your body with negative feelings will only deform it from its natural loveliness. Constant criticisms of *too much cellulite on the thighs, too much flab on the tummy, legs too short* and *arms too fat* are not helpful or constructive for the body. It is an unkind attitude, and it has unfavourable effects on our sweet body. You might feel, *if only my body was more attractive, I would feel more positive towards it*. But that is not how creative force works. The cause for any reality can never be on the outside. The power to change starts with you. If you don't give loving attention to your body, it has no loveliness to reflect back to you. Your feminine splendour can only be manifested by Love and positivity.

Unbeknown to you, you have been creating not what you want, but what you don't want. Energy follows thought. Each time you focus on any part of the body that you deem undesirable, you are energising it and keeping it in its existing state. The more you think it is unsightly, the more it will persist in staying that way. Remember how the law of attraction works?

Your body listens to every thought and emotion you have. Each thought or emotion is either filling your body with delight, from your appreciation, or despondency, from your criticisms. Your body is constantly conveying these feelings back to you. When all your body hears is how unhappy and disappointed you are about the way it is, it has no alternative but to mutate into a form of disappointment. On the other hand, if you choose to concentrate on the positive aspects of your body, appreciating what you already have, your body is more likely to respond in kind. You will also be able to see the attractiveness that a critical eye misses. Love your body and your body will respond back with beauty, it's as simple as that. Treat your body how you would like to be treated.

A JuicyWoman shows her appreciation and gratitude towards her body by taking good care of it. And when she moisturises her body, she silently affirms how special it is, and how thankful she is for all the gifts it brings. She mentally sees the body as beautiful and healthy, instead of focussing on its flaws, and somehow it begins to unfold into a form of loveliness. Such is the alchemy of Love.

Your body is hosting you,
so that you can live the fullest expression
of who you are.
How are you loving it
that it may do its job well for you?

39

Acceptance Allows Your Body
to Evolve Into Loveliness

Another important thing to know is that acceptance is a necessary precursor to any change that you want to take place in your body. In other words, whatever shape and form your body is in right now needs to be fully embraced by you before it can be any different. Until you fully accept your body for the way it is right now, there is no hope of making real changes. Many of us despise how we look to the extent that we can't even bear to look at our naked body in the mirror.

As long as we dislike our body, and consider it ugly or unattractive, the pressure and tension that come from non-acceptance will keep the body fixed in its present perceived unattractive state. The law of nature says that *the stronger we resist something, the harder it will persist.* So to release the body from this self-condemned state, it requires that we love it without conditions. If the energetic force of non-acceptance can lock this perceived unattractiveness in place, then by the same token, true acceptance and self-love can release it and allow your inherent loveliness to surface.

Most of us are not as beautiful and gorgeous as we can be. We compromise our beauty when we are being critical, when we measure ourselves against unrealistic, touched-up photos of women in magazines. To allow our innate loveliness to shine we need to:

- Stop criticising the way our body looks.
- Start to be conscious of how the mind affects and shapes the body.
- Stop comparing how we look with what we see in magazines.
- Start to appreciate how our body allows us to live and experience life.

- Show the body our appreciation by treating it well with healthy food, exercise and plenty of quality rest.
- Stop using negative language about our body. It is listening, and will respond accordingly.
- Start loving ourselves as we are. Learn to love the bits we deem unattractive. A loved body is a happy body, and a happy body will have a natural glow and exude an attractiveness that no surgery can produce.
- At night, before you close your eyes to end the day, thank your body for all the gifts it has brought you. For the adventures you have had that day. For enabling you to do everything you've done that day. And for the experience of being alive. This practice of gratitude will energise and inspire your body to do more to please you and make you happy. Every happy servant wants to serve her mistress well.

A JuicyWoman knows that for her to be the gorgeous creature that she is meant to be, the relationship between the body and mind must be healed. Any self-loathing, dissatisfaction or non-acceptance will stand in the way of healing and her potential beauty.

☙ ♥ ♥ ♥ ❧

My unhappiness
is simply a helpful gauge
to get my attention
that I need to return to my Juicy self.

☙ ♥ ♥ ♥ ❧

40

We Eat When We Are Unhappy

No animal in the wild overeats. If a tiger were to overeat and get fat, it would not be quick enough to catch its next meal when it was hungry again. Through lack of food, any excess weight drops off and the tiger is able to hunt again. Nature constantly keeps itself in balance.

Unfortunately, the same cannot be said for us, the seemingly more intelligent species. We eat when we are bored, we eat when we are unhappy and we eat even when we are not hungry! Even though we are part of this wondrous nature, we seem to have no understanding about balance, so we continue to tip the scales the wrong way—so much so that morbid obesity is now the new pandemic of modern living. And still some of us keep stuffing food into our already-gorged stomachs. What is going on?

We use food as a distraction so we can avoid having to pay attention to the unhappy feelings that well up from the murky depths of our psyche. The more dejected we feel, the more we head for the fridge. As if food will plug the emotional hole that's gaping inside us. Instead of using our sensuous mouth and tongue to kiss and express intimacy or expound wisdom, we use them to empty plates and ice cream tubs. What we excessively consume and do not use, our body stores away like a diligent storehouse manager. As those inches pile on, so does our disgust towards our body. We all know it's a no-win situation, yet we seem too weak to break the wicked spell.

Often, we do not eat because our body needs us to. We eat to numb what we are feeling. We can't bear the pain, so we eat. We can't stand the loneliness, so we eat. And each piece of chocolate, cake, biscuit or extra piece of pizza that we stuff into our belly, when digested, continues to build up a layer of unloved flesh in our body. It is not possible for unloved flesh to be attractive. As we balloon outwards, we become more deeply acquainted with the non-loving emotions that we have towards ourselves.

The unhappier we feel, the more we eat. The more weight we pile on, the more dejected we feel. The more despondent we are, the more we eat again. We have created hell-on-meals for ourselves.

The only way out is to tend to your unhappiness. Until you mend this emotional puncture, no amount of dieting will work. You will find that you will lose the weight, but then pile it on again in the not too distant future. Until you literally make your life sweet again, your sweet tooth will compel you to reach for those cakes, chocolates and biscuits. You are unconsciously using the artificial as a substitute for the real thing. It won't work. Nature will not allow us to cheat without paying a price. You need to get the puncture kit out and start mending.

Suppose every excess pound on my body equates to a pound of my unhappiness, discontentment or frustration, and it's simply knocking on my door seeking my loving attention. Instead of habitually reaching out for food, let me stop and listen. *What is depressing my joy? How am I not expressing my truth? What areas in my life make me feel unsatisfied?* If you are not able to identify clearly the cause of these unhappy feelings, seek professional help. Instead of eating your way through your unhappiness, the most loving action is to seek help. It is spiritual food that you need. It is your spiritual radiance that you're after. Be kind to yourself. Take the time to sort out your emotional issues. Whatever they may be, they're not a big deal. You can use them as a fuel to feed the fire of your soul. Every obstacle is simply a blessed step to take us closer to the summit of our gorgeous splendour. We live in fortunate times that the world is full of good counsellors, coaches and mentors. We need support if we are to function happily in this fast-moving society. There is no longer a stigma attached to seeking help. Don't wait any longer to take a more loving route towards healing yourself. You deserve the best that love and life have to offer you.

A JuicyWoman will not bury herself in food or other distractions if there is an issue to be sorted out. She will devote her attention to straightening every twist or kink that stops her joy from manifesting. She knows she deserves to be happy.

≈ ❤ ❤ ❤ ≈

Let all my movement gently yield
something of Love.

≈ ❤ ❤ ❤ ≈

41

When Your Body Flows, You Glow

As little girls, our body moved with lightness. Jumping up and down for joy delighted not only our little heart, but those around us too. When the rhythm moved us, we would wiggle and sway happily. Life would surge its joy through us and we wouldn't object. We had no internal complications to stop us from being animated by what thrills us.

Now, such simplicity and liberty feel like lifetimes ago. This sense of freedom and ease of being in our female body feels unfamiliar now. Many of us have forgotten how to take delight from simply being in our body. Most of the time, our physical frame is locked in stereotype movements. We walk, sit, stand or lie. That's as good as it gets. No more leaping with delight. No more pirouetting with joy. No more being compelled to lie in beautiful meadows. Even when we dance, the movements are safe, predictable and controlled.

We no longer inhabit our body fully. We use it rather than live in it. Day in, day out, the body is manoeuvred to serve our mundane purposes. We have forgotten how to let our gorgeous body echo the meaning of life for us. It doesn't look how we want it to look either. It is our most faithful friend and we don't even recognise it.

The rigidity of our thinking shows up as rigidity in our body. Constant fear and tension causes our body to be stiff and inflexible. As we lose our ability to bend with the winds of change, we lose our suppleness too. And as we lose our suppleness, we also lose our zest for adventure. The unpredictable unnerves us and the unknown frightens us. We hide in our comfort zone, never meeting our bold, daring and audacious self.

If we need to be reminded how gracefully we can move, watch nature. Nature is the pure embodiment of the feminine essence. Whether a running brook or a bird flying through the air, an ebbing tide or a tree gently swaying in the breeze, nature shows us what moving without resistance looks like—sheer enchantment. She shows us what dancing without fear looks like—pure elation. Opposing nothing, she moves and dances with everything that comes her way. She is forever open and giving. That is why no soul can resist the beauty of nature. We flock to places of extraordinary natural beauty to bask in her enchantment.

The same goes for a woman. Nothing is more attractive and pleasing to a man than a happy woman whose feminine body flows when she moves. Nothing is more captivating than a woman whose walk and gestures embody the fullness of her love and integrity. To reclaim our gracefulness, we need to loosen the grip of fear. Fear does not protect us or keep us safe. Love does. Let's stop numbing ourselves and let's start feeling again. Let's be honest with who we are and let the world take pleasure in our quirkiness. Let's not hold back our passion and blaze forth the light of who we are.

A JuicyWoman would feel free to gyrate and shake her delicious hips, be it on the dancefloor or in the way she lives her life. Sexy and potent, she sways and unashamedly undulates her lovely female form. She does it, not so much to seduce others, but because she feels the utter pleasure of being a woman. Letting go of guilt and fear, she is free to delight in her own sensuousness. Her body flows with ease, whatever the circumstance, enchanting all with her feminine radiance.

Your Juicy Relationship With Man

za ❤ ❤ ❤ za

How do I live each moment
totally open as Love
in touch with my innermost soul
and giving my deepest gifts
to my beloved?

za ❤ ❤ ❤ za

42

If You Say You Hate Men
or Would Rather Be Single,
It's Only Because You're Hurting Inside

What we say reflects the story that's going on in our head. When we listen beyond the spoken words, the face value of what's being said, this inner psycho-drama is quickly revealed. So what is really going on when we say that men are bastards, good-for-nothing losers, we hate them and we would rather be single? It shouts in bright, red-blooded letters that we have been deeply hurt by them. It screams of unresolved pain and mistrust towards men. This hostility towards men is a mask to cover up our unhealed wounds in our intimate relationships, past or present, and ultimately the non-loving beliefs we have about ourselves.

We are born to love. In spite of our pain and fear, our need for love will always drive us towards a relationship, no matter how hard we convince ourselves we're happier without one. Many of us find relationships challenging at the best of times. Dealing with our own insecurities and neuroses is tiring enough, so coping with our partner's hang-ups and problems frustrates us even further. We project our own fear onto the other and see the other as the obstacle to our happiness and joy. Eventually, we stop relating altogether, especially on an intimate level.

This is why some people find loving animals much easier. For a start, they don't argue back, and they always seem grateful for whatever little acts of kindness they get from us. They certainly don't criticise or upset us emotionally, so that makes us relax and be open with them. Animals are great demonstrators of unconditional love, and their consistent affection and openness can be an excellent tonic for our cautious heart.

After the breakdown of an intense and difficult relationship, it's always good and necessary to take time to recover and heal before we jump into the next one. Being on your own will give you the psychic space, to learn from the mess, to take responsibility for your part of the dysfunction, and to clear the debris before you invite the next beloved in. But if a woman insists that she doesn't need to be in an intimate relationship, while she hates being on her own, it's usually because she is afraid of being hurt or let down by a man. Those who say they don't need it are often the ones who need it most. They need the mirror an intimate relationship provides, from which to see their unconscious patterns of non-love towards themselves. Once they clear these unhealthy patterns, they will find intimate relationships uncomplicated and effortless.

Many of us struggle to get on with the man in our life. This is because he is the uncompromising mirror from which we see our hidden fears and self-judgements. He shows us clearly where we have divorced ourselves from our own heart, for to get on with the other is to get on with oneself. To love and adore the other is devotion towards the sacred within.

A JuicyWoman knows that she has no option but to tear open her vulnerability, if she is to be ravished by Love. She accepts that every emotional wound has to be dealt with and healed if she is to be her true, radiant, feminine self. Her relationship with her beloved is a spiritual practice to discover the Love she already is, but has momentarily forgotten.

ᰀ ❤ ❤ ❤ ᰀ

There is no such thing
as being with the wrong man.
There is only having the wrong beliefs
about yourself.

ᰀ ❤ ❤ ❤ ᰀ

43

The Man You're With Reflects
How You Feel About Yourself

If you want to know how you really feel about yourself, take a look at the man you are with. How he treats you is the mirror in which to see what you think of yourself.

If he doesn't respect you, it's because on a subconscious level, you don't respect yourself. If he treats you like a housekeeper it could be because you feel it's your job to be one because he can't be bothered to lift his finger to help. If you feel he is using you and yet you still do everything for him, this is because you have an unconscious need to be useful. Your belief system thinks you can buy love through being useful. You get your self-worth from being needed. While you rage in your resentment that he won't get off his backside to help you, you get the payback from feeling self-righteous and superior because you are the one that gets things done. And until you stop treating him like a child, he won't stop behaving like an imbecile either.

He will treat you like an angel if you believe you are one yourself, with or without wings. And when you remember you own gorgeousness and deep beauty, a beauty not only pleasing to the eye but also a face and body shaped by compassion and kindness, he will see appreciate you like a beautiful flower.

But if he starts verbalising that you look fat and that he doesn't find you sexy anymore, start the journey to find your self-esteem and self worth right away because you have lost them somewhere along the line in the relationship. You don't need to kill him for hurting your feelings. Thank him instead for bringing your self-neglect to your attention.

We are always with the 'right' man, the man whose gifts serve as the mirror in which we can see our hidden beliefs clearly.

One woman was puzzled that man after man in her intimate relationships would start out treating her like a princess, full of praise and in awe of her clever ways, but after a while they would become aggressive towards her to the point of being physically intimidating. She couldn't understand why. What she couldn't see was her own attacking behaviour towards them. Disguised in undertones of therapy language, she would constantly point out their faults, the areas in which they could improve, what they should do, what they shouldn't have done, and on and on it went. *Emasculate a man long enough and you can guarantee yourself a raging monster in return!* Unless you're Empress Dowager (a powerful Chinese Empress who relished in having eunuchs in her court), you cannot chop off a man's balls and expect him to still want to keep you on a pedestal. He will be in too much psychic pain to contemplate being sweet and tender towards you! We have no idea of the power we yield, so we tend to misuse it. In the case of this woman, no matter how many times she swapped the man for a new one, they always ended up being abusive towards her. The woman believes she deserves attack, and so by harassing her man, she gets attacked in return.

Some women feel they tend to end up with men who are losers. Somewhere deep inside they must have 'loser' attitudes to attract them in. *Birds of a feather? Like attracts like?* We've heard it all before, so it's time to pay attention if you're one of these women. Don't dump him to get a new one. You'll only be exchanging for more of the same. You will find another hundred like him, waiting to offer you the same 'gifts'. Just sort yourself out. Find your confidence. Improve your self-esteem. Start the all-important inner journey to track your JuicyWoman down—she's in there somewhere. And when she surfaces, your whole world will be different. Your beast could well be a prince in disguise.

Like nature, we evolve and change through time; we may not be the same woman who started out in our intimate relationship. Hopefully, we have grown spiritually and changed for the better as our understanding has deepened. And hopefully, our partner mirrors this change in us too.

If two people in a relationship endeavour to always maintain heart-to-heart communication with each other, they do tend to progress at the same rate. But if in your relationship you only talk about practical and mundane matters, your tender hearts never get to meet, so neither of you has a clue who the other person really is, other than your own projected ideas of each other. When that's the case, you're both in trouble, because there is no trust in the relationship. Real solid trust comes from a steady knowing of each other. And as you leave your caterpillar cocoon behind and evolve into the most gorgeous butterfly, with trust, your man will not be threatened by this awesome change in you. Instead, he will be inspired and want the same freedom for himself, and both of you will soar to greater heights together.

A JuicyWoman knows that if she feels un-nurtured in her relationship with her man, she needs to investigate why she is neglecting her own needs. She understands that her man is only a reflected image of her deep beliefs about herself. When she improves her relationship with her sweet self, her man will treat her differently.

*You fight men
when you're at war with yourself.*

*All fighting will cease to be
when you fall in Love with yourself.*

181

44

There is No War with Man

The battle of the sexes! Man versus Woman! War cries can be heard ringing in the psyche of most women. For many of us, these cries are so subtle that we don't even know we are at war. But our psychic body seems to show deep cuts, swollen bruises and scarred wounds for it.

"Men are jerks and I'm better off without them"
"You can never trust a man"
"Men leave their partner for a younger woman"
"Men are such bullies"
"You know what men are like – useless!"

Every time such statements are muttered, or even thought, we are attacking men. You hear it slipping out of your friends' lips, or your own, and think nothing of it. Deriding men with our girlfriends as we roll our eyes and tut with disapproval may momentarily ease the pent-up frustration or feelings of resentment brewing away inside us, but it will not make our life easier or better. Neither will it resolve the conflicts and confusion we have. It will only serve to weaken men and make us feel we're pathetic creatures, at the mercy of unloving, uncaring men. This outlook is totally divisive.

As society at large is still patriarchal in nature, it is more comfortable for us women to think that it is men who are to blame for the problems we have in the world. That way, we don't have to look at our own part in it all. It is also easier to think the problems we have at home as the fault of the man we're with, so that we can deny our responsibility in the partnership. It doesn't take much for a woman to see the man as the oppressor either, since he is physically stronger but it's our place to set the moral standards of the world.

We have such thoughts partly because feminism has encouraged us to think that we have to fight men in order to have what should have been our birthright. Seething away in our psyche is an unquestioned thought that says our standing in this world depends on how well we fight men. We think that if we have what men have, we will be happy. So we strive for the top job and the fat bonuses. We try to give ourselves the same sexual liberties. *If a man can sleep around, why can't I? A man can be ruthless in getting what he wants, so why shouldn't I do the same?* We invent the 'top bitch' syndrome and silently delight in the fear we generate as we crack the whip and drive our subordinates into hell holes. We go against our own feminine grain and become aggressive. We erroneously believe we have to be hard in order to be effective.

This need to compete and fight with men has cost us dearly, especially in parenthood. While a man can father children well into his eighties and beyond, we have our biological clock to consider. Where is the equality in that? We are now living in an era where countless career women regret leaving their maternal needs too late. Years of putting career first and getting caught up in the 'having it all' syndrome has caused our feminine body to renegade and deny these women the joy of motherhood. We have to be careful that we are not on the front line fighting a battle we can't win. Women need to wise up and start questioning if the road feminism has put us on is one that serves our happiness.

It is becoming clearer that behaving as men do is not the way to achieve our deepest joy. This fight for equality, this war with men, has confused them, and the price we pay is the way they treat us—like another man, rather than a captivating woman who enchants their heart. We must wake up to what is staring us in the face—that 'having it all', men's way, doesn't work for women.

Let's try a new way instead. Let's try having it all, the woman's way. Let's make a point of not making another derogatory remark towards our man, and all men in general. Let's not attack them by running them down. Instead of assailing them with our unkind thoughts or our harsh words, let's focus on their good qualities instead. Instead of harping on about their weaknesses, let's concentrate on their strengths. As his powerful counterpart, you need to give him gentle help and encouragement in order to bring out the best in him. Do it for his sake, as well as your own.

A JuicyWoman is intelligent enough to see that nature hasn't made a mistake by putting men and women together in the same pot. Fighting and attacking men will only make a bad stew. We are meant to get along. We are meant to complement each other in the most beautiful way. When we do, the feast of life begins.

ક- ❤ ❤ ❤ ક-

Like water
your softness is your strength
that influences everything it touches.

Like water
your softness is the liquid light
that dissolves all conflicts it meets.

ક- ❤ ❤ ❤ ક-

45

Your Softness is Your Greatness

Being hard is not an intrinsic part of our feminine essence. Men love us for the softness of our lips, the softness of our body and the softness of our feminine nature. Men have never *loved* us when we were hard. When a woman is being demanding, unyielding and controlling, she loses her radiance and becomes unattractive.

A woman is meant to nurture life, not crush it. When we are ruthless, we go against our feminine nature and flow. This has a serious effect on our wellbeing. It kills us rather than enlivens us.

When we stop mimicking men, and have the courage to embody and live our feminine essence, to use understanding instead of force, and to use Love instead of fear, we will be able to bring about the much-needed change in our society. In the workplace, feminine principles like genuine care and support for one another will then be the norm, rather than the back-stabbing, cruel bitching behaviour we see at the moment.

It is not realistic to expect men to instigate this change. Their journey, although parallel, is not the same as ours. It is up to us to show the way back to Love, by being the example. By believing in the power of kindness. Not by showing kindness, but by being kindness itself. By living, breathing and walking as kindness.

When you understand the dynamics and energies of the principles of the Masculine and the Feminine, you will see that Woman is the softer sex. She is the yielding force of the universe. By yielding, we don't mean giving in to a man's whims and fancies. By yielding, we mean to be like water, a pure, liquid light of love that can penetrate into the most reluctant corner. The power of such softness can flow into any container and take its shape without losing its own identity. It doesn't fight or resist. It gives in, in order to influence. Just like the ocean, it gently claims everything back to itself.

There is nothing weak at all in our softness. Being soft doesn't mean we let people walk all over us. Being soft doesn't mean we become hand towels for people to wipe their grime on. Being soft means we use love and kindness to inspire and to win over resistance. Being soft also means we are not afraid to be vulnerable. Vulnerable is attractive because it's honest. It automatically endears hearts to reach out and give the helping hand that's needed.

When we need to say 'no', we can say it with a soft smile. It's more effective than tensing your body and saying it with a hard face. Tender softness is very disarming indeed. Staying beautifully gentle, we can still be firm in upholding our feminine principles—to love, to nurture and to enliven life.

There is no need to compete with or emulate men. The masculine essence is different from the feminine. Having what men have will not fulfil us. Having what men have will drive us further away from our true nature. We will become less desirable, and our dreams to love, to be loved and to be seen in our radiance will remain unrealised. A woman who loves deeply, who gives life and joy and radiates the beauty of life, is a great woman. Only such a woman can heal discord back into harmony. Only such a woman feels truly contented. Only such a woman feels blessed to be a woman. This accolade has been beckoning every woman from the moment she was born.

A JuicyWoman sees her softness as strength. She knows that being hard and busting balls, especially in the workplace, will only make her grow her own. She has no desire to be like a man. She relishes the pleasure and delight of being a woman far too much to go against her own grain. She also knows it is not necessary. She excels in everything she does by simply being soft and feminine, the way nature has intended her to be.

❧ ❤ ❤ ❤ ❧

In Love
is where a man matures into his greatness
and a woman blossoms into her splendour.

❧ ❤ ❤ ❤ ❧

46

Woman + Man = Yoga of Love

Couples get together for different reasons. For most, it's something you do because you have reached a certain age—get together, have the house and the two-point-five children. Some do it out of convenience or because it makes good financial sense. For others, it's because they are emotionally needy and are terrified of being on their own. In fact, most see relationships as something to take from, rather than something to give to. Rare are those who actually enter a relationship as a spiritual practice, as an art-form, as yoga—to master and learn about love. Missing this crucial point, we end up being disappointed, disillusioned and frustrated in the relationship.

Rare are couples who have no bones to pick with each other, rarer still are couples who adore each other completely. Most find intimate relationships hard going, stressful and frustrating. This is so because we are coming into it with the wrong intent—to take, rather than to give. Most relationships are afflicted by the 'give me' syndrome. Give me love. Give me a baby. Give me sex. Give me your money. Give me a bigger house. Give me luxurious holidays. These are the obvious examples. The more subtle examples would be: give me your approval, give me your appreciation, give me validation, give me assurance, and so on. It is a senseless hunger that can never be satisfied. Why? Because nothing can come from the outside if it is not found on the inside first.

You are always in the perfect relationship, one that is perfect for your growth. You are each other's mirror, in which you see clearly your relationship with yourself. With your partner, you get to see what you haven't given to yourself. If you find that you're always looking for him to assure you that he loves you, then you have yet to love yourself. And until you do, no matter how many times he tells you he does, you won't believe him. When you love yourself, the whole world will adore you as well.

Most women enter into a relationship with a man with armfuls of expectations and wishful thinking. With the 'knight in shining amour' firmly embedded in her psyche, a woman goes into the relationship expecting the man to fulfil all her needs. We expect him to make us happy. We expect him to make us feel special. We expect him to adore us no matter how mean we are to him. We expect him to always do the right thing. We expect him to accept our neurosis and still be in love with us. All these unrealistic expectations mean we set ourselves up for disappointments. No one can give us what we must give ourselves.

A relationship is a spiritual gym, a place where we have constant opportunities to exercise those weak love-muscles in us, until they become super strong in the art of loving. A relationship is also the self-erasing canvas on which we keep practising our masterstrokes until we produce a masterpiece of love. Through this, we get to become fierce in our loving. Withholding nothing and resisting nothing, we come to be true masters of Love. That is a tremendous gift that relationships bring.

A relationship is also a necessity, because it is the means by which we realise who we are—the radiance of Love itself. It is a necessity because, through it, we come to know that we are not the person we think we are. What is left is a gorgeous, divine creature whose Love knows no bounds.

A relationship is a sacred container holding two souls together, in the name of Love, while they go through the growing pains, individually and with each other. When bound by Love and trust, they evolve and grow into their finest selves. The nurturing qualities in an intimate relationship have the same effect as the sun and rain have on a seed—the woman blossoms into her feminine splendour, while the man matures into his majestic greatness. And only when we see the sanctity that a relationship brings will we be able to unearth every single joy, delight and pleasure awaiting us and our beloved. Conflict, confusion and frustration will become a thing of the past.

A JuicyWoman sees her relationship with her man as a yoga for Love, a sacred practice in which she works on the suppleness of her heart and mind. With regular practice, the Love she is shines through and she remembers who she is—a divine woman, with the privilege of loving a divine man. When a woman remembers her splendour, a good man can barely contain his joy. His true self arises in her benevolent presence.

꒜ ❤ ❤ ❤ ꒜

If you want to put a man off
- be easy.

If you want to enchant your man
- hold on to your integrity.

꒜ ❤ ❤ ❤ ꒜

47

Being Too Easy is a Big Turn-off

In the dating scene these days, women often make the gravest mistake—they make it too easy for the man. With our so-called equality mindset, we think it is okay to make the first move. If a man takes our fancy, we approach him. We think nothing of asking for his number and ringing him for a date. And if, after a couple of meetings, he has not called back, we text him or ring him. Our financial independence has boosted our confidence, and in our eagerness to have the same 'rights' as men, to do as they do, we're quite happy to play the masculine role in courtship. With our own bare hands, we voluntarily rip away at our enchanting mystique and smash our feminine appeal to smithereens. No wonder he's staying away.

We forget one vital point—that there is a Neolithic hunter in every good man. The thrill of spending hours stalking his rare find, and the immense satisfaction he gets when he finally nets his hard-earned prize, is beyond our female comprehension. Nothing rocks his world more than succeeding in a difficult challenge. Ladies, take note and wise up. If you do all the work for him, he will lie back, take your gifts, and then chuck you out with his half-eaten pizzas. Easy come, easy go.

Even though we may live in an ultra-modern world, when it comes to courtship there is a primal ritual that we need to understand and respect. In the courtship dance, if the woman is doing the pursuing, she emasculates the man. A man's need for dominance is essential if he is a good, wholesome man. Only when a man displays his strength to overcome will a woman trust him. The act of pursuing his chosen mate should begin with her rejecting his advances. The more she plays hard to get, the more interested and fascinated he becomes. He enjoys the challenge of not knowing if he will succeed in winning her over. It makes him work harder and apply himself, stretching his creative means.

Through that, he gets to feel his potency. This affirms his manhood and makes him feel good. It spurs him on to continue the chase and eventually, if the chemistry is right, the woman opens her heart to accept his advances. His perseverance has invoked a sense of trust in her. She is happy to yield into his arms because he has shown his integrity and genuine interest towards her through his persistence, patience and effort. This process is essential for all male and female creatures in nature. Except for the odd spider, there is no exception. We would do well to learn from it. When we women ditch this natural process, we end up with a dejected heart, waiting by the phone for a call that never comes.

Next is the sex bit. Sleeping with a man before he gets the chance to know you beyond the smell of your pheromones is a bad, bad idea. You're thinking: *He seems nice, and if I give him sex he will give me his heart, or at least a visitor's pass to start with?* Not so. If you sleep with a man before his emotions get a chance to kick in, to develop some feelings towards you, his relationship with you can only be about sex. He will only know the feel of your skin, the contours of your flesh and the way you sigh with pleasure, which incidentally isn't that different from most other women. If you don't make him wait long enough to discover how passionately you feel about the food crisis in Tajikistan, how a tiny house spider can make you run into his arms, and your other adorable idiosyncrasies, you'll be just another pleasure doll for him. And he won't be building a pleasure house for dolly to live in. That isn't how men work.

But if I put my foot on the brake, he might think I'm a bore and take his attention elsewhere. This is a fear that can drive a woman to give too much, too quickly in the beginning. You sleep with him in the hope that having sex will shoot out invisible tendrils to bind him to you. No chance. Sleeping with him too soon only deprives him of the incentive to want to get to know you better.

So if we are smart, Juicy women, we will not be easy, go fast or cut short the courtship. After all, being wooed is one of the most delightful experiences for a woman on planet earth. Of course, being adored and deeply loved is the best, and that comes when we have done the first bit right.

A JuicyWoman lets a man know she likes him, but never shows that she is keen. Even if he was George Clooney or Brad Pitt, she would never betray her feminine soul by being too easy or accommodating. She knows that a man who is worth her attention is one who has earned the right to her heart through his own merit and strength of character.

8 ❤ ❤ ❤ 8

Rush to have sex with a man
and he will rush you
out of his life.

8 ❤ ❤ ❤ 8

48

More Reasons Why You Should Not Rush to Bed

If you let a man have his way, he will have no qualms about sleeping with you before he even finds out your surname. Male sexual instincts are wired differently from ours. In general, a man is more *objective* towards sex, and he can have the hots for you without being at all interested in you as a person. Once the conquest is made, his attention moves on. We, on the other hand, tend to relate to sex from our emotional centre, making sex a *subjective* experience. We need to like the person he is. And often, we're keener on the man after having slept with him. We want to know that he likes us, and we often want to take the relationship further.

How long should you wait before you sleep with the man you're seeing? *The longer the better.* If you want a guideline, if you meet Mr Handsome at the start of winter, wait until the first oak leaf appears before you let him into your inner chamber. If he's too impatient and threatens to go somewhere else before lady spring arrives, he's not really into you. Keep your knickers on. No loss. You've been spared. Your cherished feminine honour will be intact for when the real one shows up.

Avoid sleeping with him until he has the chance to develop genuine feelings for you. Because no matter how hot the sex is, when the sexual thrill is over and he's back on planet sober, you'll be a stranger in his bed and he will have nothing to build on with you. If he's to take you seriously, he needs more than just sexual attraction to sustain his interest once he has satisfied his carnal urge. He needs time to get to know you intellectually, emotionally and personally.

Apparently, a man sees more clearly how he really feels towards a woman just after ejaculation. Before sex, his interest in her is intensely coloured by his sexual desire. But as he lies back in post-coital mode, no longer distracted by the stirrings in his loins, the truth about his feelings becomes more obvious to him. This is when he decides if you're just a good-time girl or a woman worthy of his pursuit. If he doesn't have much to go by, you'll just be another hit and run to him.

If we love the woman we are, we won't sleep with a man until we know he's the type of man we want to have a serious relationship with. We wouldn't want him to think we're easy. It is no good telling him that you don't usually jump into bed with others as quickly as you have just done with him. He won't feel special, and neither will he be convinced. Your *'I can't get my knickers off quick enough'* approach shouts much louder than anything you say!

Here's the secret. The man actually likes it if you make him wait. First, he won't be thinking that you're a common carp that can be hooked by anyone with bait on his rod. Men like the thought that they have managed to pull in an enchanting mermaid, a rare kind, one that no other man has ever had the good fortune to deserve. The level of enjoyment and satisfaction is as different as getting a quick hamburger at a greasy takeaway or dining at a sophisticated restaurant with a long waiting list. The latter wins, hands down.

A smart woman will not rush to have sex, no matter how horny she feels. She controls her desires as she knows that giving in to a man too quickly is like throwing away her trump card. Such a move will compromise her standing with the man. There's no doubt that you have a man's full attention when he hasn't got what he wants from you yet. He will be most attentive and eager to know you. He may not be able to keep his hands off you but, as you insist he does, he will hold you in high esteem and regard. Not only does he not mind waiting, he actually prefers it.

Attractive men have this notion that they only have to say please and the woman will comply. Perhaps we're desperate to be desired. Or perhaps we see it as an equality thing—if they can be casual about sex, so can we; if they can use us for sex, so can we. But this outlook is detrimental to our feminine essence. By being sexually easy, we send men the wrong message—that they don't need to make any effort with us.

What happens is that romance dies. Why should he send you flowers or wine and dine you when he can pop over with a movie and have sex with you before the night is over?

Just as every little girl loves fairytales, every feminine woman loves romance. In romance we feel special. In romance we glow and feel desired. In romance our heart flutters with delight. But rushing into sex before he allows you into his heart, is the surest way of killing the romance. Why deprive yourself of such gorgeous pleasures?

The minute you sleep with a man, the dynamic between you changes. Once we have shared intimacy, the man tends to feel more sure of himself, while we feel more vulnerable. And if you don't have the emotional closeness to fall back on after sex, the morning after can feel terribly awkward. While you're looking for telltale signs that he wants to see you again, his mind could be racing to come up with the best excuse he can think of to get you out of the door. He might soften the blow by saying he'll ring you, and he might do if he fancies more easy sex with you, but that's it. Don't expect him to want more from you. By jumping into bed too quickly with a man, you are telling him that you don't think much of yourself. So why would he think much of you either? If you feel you need to sleep with him in order to win him over, he will sense it and lose respect for you. It is for a man to win over a woman, not the other way round.

A JuicyWoman knows it is smarter to make a man wait before sleeping with him. She understands that this appeals to his hunter's instinct, and to let him have his catch too easily is to make him lose interest in her too soon. She is also aware that the time gap between meeting a man and sleeping with him is a valuable period where the man learns how the woman wants to be treated. And, being a smart woman, she wouldn't compromise this by rushing into sex with him, no matter how irresistible he may be. She appreciates that making a man wait is a sign of elegance.

❧ ❤ ❤ ❤ ❧

*When you become the right woman
you will attract the right man.*

❧ ❤ ❤ ❤ ❧

49

Successful, but Can't Attract the Right Man

Many successful women moan that they can't find the right guy. Or if they do, they can't seem to keep him. Contrary to women's belief, there isn't a shortage of good men in this world, and yes, they do come unattached too. So why can't these clever women magnetise a wonderful man, and make him want to spend the rest of his life with them?

Many would say that men are threatened by a successful woman, that they are emasculated by her accomplishments and her 'can do' outlook. Investigating deeper, we see that this is not true. Men are not threatened by our success; they are put off by certain attitudes that we, as high achievers, often have.

Being good at our job may mean we can sweat the big stuff like our counterparts in suits. Perhaps we got to the top because we know how to bust balls to achieve the necessary results. We take charge, we direct, we give constructive criticism and we even fire subordinates if they don't measure up. We are more likely to be respected, feared or hated, or all three at the same time. One thing for sure is we won't be loved. That's fine in the office, but bad news when we take this approach home to our personal life.

To lead requires that we slip into our masculine persona. No matter how feminine a woman is, the moment she takes charge, her femininity fades into oblivion behind the deep folds of her heart, while her masculine side leaps to the front to run the show. This is the law of polarity—you are embodying one or the other, but *you can't be both feminine and masculine at the same time.* It will serve us well to remember this fact. If you are leading, directing, controlling, you are in your masculine energy. And that means your feminine essence is tucked away somewhere in the recess of your being and can only emerge when your masculine takes a back seat. Unfortunately, when we don't understand the different dynamics and qualities of the masculine and feminine principles, we tend to identify stronger with our 'I'm in charge' personality, partly because we believe that is the only way to get what we want. This 'I'm the boss' attitude might be effective at work, but it won't manifest what our heart deeply desires in our intimate life. Unless you're a woman who always wants to be on top of your man, in or out of the bedroom, and you want a boy rather than a man to share your life with, open your mind and start making some changes. 'Miss I'm In Control' will not meet 'Mr I Will Ravish You With Love'.

We need to see that we wear this 'I'm tough, don't mess with me' uniform because we believe it protects us. Our strong exterior is only a form of defence, so no one will hurt us. We install this 'Major General' at the forefront because beneath our hard exterior there are wounds that need to be healed. And heal them we must if we are to let our feminine heart live her dream. Once healed, we will be happy to trust life again, and when we trust, we are at ease being open, soft and vulnerable, and all the feminine traits that men love and delight in.

But when we're marching in our masculinity, we don't endear ourselves to men. They might respect us, but if you're a feminine woman, that's not really what you want. Mills & Boon books and the like don't fly off the shelves because the hero 'respects' the heroine. Respect is okay, but it doesn't rock our feminine soul. What our feminine heart wants more than anything is to be *ravished* and *die* in Love. Don't panic, what dies here is not you, but your fears and everything that stands in the way of your joy. The feminine *loves* surrendering into the arms of Love. And you can only do that when you cultivate trust in your man, and men in general. And you can only do that when you have healed what you're afraid of.

Men *love* relaxing in the soft feminine. That's why they rush off to beautiful places, because nature is feminine. One of the gifts of the feminine is that she relaxes all those who come into her fold. A self-assured man who is in touch with his purpose, and successful in what he does, is not drawn to masculine energy. He already has plenty of his own. What he finds compelling, and irresistible, is the soft feminine.

To a man, there is nothing more attractive than a feminine woman who is soft and open, happy and expressive in her delights. We don't realise how potently we can disarm a man when our voice is soft, our body relaxed and our face a smiling joy. More can be achieved with this feminine approach than you can ever imagine. A man so loves to please us when we are our happy self. They are captivated by our radiance.

A confident, wholesome man who is already efficient in directing his own life does not need a controlling woman. He will not find her domineering streak appealing. Only a boy would want a woman to show him the way and coerce him into action. Only a boy would want a woman to mother him all the time. If you are attracted to juvenile men, it is because you feel more secure being in control of the relationship. Beneath your strong exterior is a frightened girl who wants to be loved and cared for, but does not believe she can have it. Until you deal with this fear, of not trusting men and, ultimately, not trusting life, you will never attract the man you want.

Good men do like strong women. There is nothing wrong with us being smart, intelligent, knowing what we want and going for it with our talent and ability. A real man is not threatened by that at all. In fact, he loves seeing a woman flourish and being happy. A confident, relaxed and self-assured woman who is also not afraid to be vulnerable is very sexy indeed to a man. Our vulnerability brings out the protective instinct in him. Any psychologically sound man who enjoys taking care of his woman will find her vulnerability alluring. It makes him want to sweep her up in his strong arms and keep her safe forever. This trust attracts her to his masculine heart. The more feminine we are, the more masculine he becomes—another aspect of the law of polarity. Playing by its rules, we will find it easy to get the best out of each other.

When we are caught up with being a successful woman at work, we also develop an unhelpful streak that prevents us from identifying the right man. We become more intolerant and less accepting of what we see as imperfections in our potential partner. Our intolerance blinds us to his good qualities. In fact, we don't hang around long enough for them to show up. So many of us have chucked away a perfectly good diamond, having mistaken it for an ordinary rock! Our closed mind and impatience could well have cost us our beloved because we didn't spot him even when he was right under our very nose.

A JuicyWoman knows that if she is to meet her beloved, she must surrender the need to take charge or be in control when she is with men. She may be efficient and authoritative at work, but once she steps out of the workplace, her masculine traits are left behind in the office. She quickly dives back into her feminine self, knowing that it is the woman and not the man in her that will attract her loved one.

ಜ 💙 💙 💙 ಜ

Rushing the courtship is like
inviting a stranger to live in your house,
sharing your bank account,
allowing him to sleep with you
and unloading his problems
before you know you're compatible.

ಜ 💙 💙 💙 ಜ

50

Take Your Time to Suss Him Out

Rushing through the dating process so you can settle down with a man quickly is as smart as giving your bank details to someone you have just met. *Of course I wouldn't do something as stupid as that,* you might exclaim. Yet time and time again, women rush to open the front door of their life and invite the man in to stay—happily ever after, or so they thought—before they find out what sort of a creature he really is. Why do we have a tendency to rush this vital process? Is it because:

- I don't like being without a man?
- I feel a lesser woman without a man?
- I want to play 'happy families' as he seems to like my children?
- My life is not complete unless I am in a relationship?
- He might change his mind if I don't tie him down quick?
- A better woman might come along?

In relationships, women tend to move things on more quickly than men do, especially on an emotional level. (If you have a man who wants that more than you, beware. He could be a needy guy who wants a mummy.) Being female also means we tend to be influenced by our emotions. When we're in love, we're floating on thin air, so it's good to be aware that our judgement might be a tad unreliable. With millions of feel-good hormones coursing through our bloodstream, it is unrealistic to expect our brain to deliver pure level-headedness and clarity of thought. We're vulnerable at this stage and would do well not to entirely trust what our eyes see or what our mind tells us. At this point, a woman's ability to discern is in selective mode. She will only hear what she wants to hear, and she will only pay attention to what she wants to see. Anything else that might burst her pink bubble will be ignored. Her powers of perception are likely to be unreliable at this stage of the game. We are more apt to disregard any gut feeling that casts the man in a negative light. We will even pretend to be blind and not give any consideration to the 'uh oh' red light, flashing up on our radar to warn us about him.

During this in-love stage, our behaviour is often out of character. Men are usually extra attentive, extra generous and extra patient, while we are extra sweet, extra tolerant and extra understanding. This is the time when the woman can wholeheartedly sympathise with the man for his problems with his ex. While he feigns interest in her chick-flick collection, she pretends to care about his football team doing well in the league. Both hide their not-so-attractive qualities and flaunt their super-good selves to capture the other's attention and to keep the interest going.

At this stage of the proceedings, we are not dealing with the norm. The norm takes time to show itself. This is why we need to be smart and stretch the courtship out for as long as possible. It is imperative that we give ourselves time to suss the guy out. Time is your best friend because:

- You need to find out if he's married or has a girlfriend.

- You need to find out about his history with women, and the way he has conducted himself in previous relationships, because we women are intelligent enough to know that men don't change. They may regulate their behaviour to get the results they want, but fundamentally they will stay as they are. If he has a history of problematic relationships, you would be wise to expect yours to end up the same. If he tells you that his exes are to be blamed, chances are you might be the next 'stupid cow' to join the line.

- You need to find out if he treats his mother and sisters well. His relationship with these women will tell you how he feels about women in general.

- You need to know what kind of creature he is. Only when you have been with him for a while can you be sure that he is not 'Mr Going Nowhere' or 'Mr Needs Fixing'.

- You need to find out if the two of you are compatible. Do you want the same things with regards to lifestyle, children, etc..? Do you share similar values about the things that matter? Do you have the same spiritual outlook? All these are important questions, and the answers are revealed not by what he says, but by how he shows himself over time.

Hurrying through this courting stage could mean more mess to clear up once he's gotten through the door and you find out he's not the one. If you have children from an earlier relationship, it will be an emotional upheaval for them to break their bond with him. Having bad run-ins with men also affects our ability to trust them. We become defensive and overly cautious in our dealings with them. This suspicious and distrustful outlook hides our gorgeous light, which is naturally there when we are open and relaxed. When that happens, our ability to draw in the one who is right for us is compromised.

A JuicyWoman knows that if she allows a man to get through the door and settle in too quickly, she is robbing herself of the chance to be properly wooed and courted. She refuses to undermine her own value. She can see that men prize their catch according to the effort they have to make. Nothing feels more exquisite to a JuicyWoman than to be truly desired by the right man. She is intelligent enough to appreciate that only time will reveal if he is indeed the right one.

❧ ♥ ♥ ♥ ❧

Being needed and being loved
is as different as mud and chocolate.

❧ ♥ ♥ ♥ ❧

51

If He Needs Rescuing, He is Still a Boy

We are such suckers when it comes to men with a sob story. *He struggles with life because his mother left without a word when he was nine.* Ah. So that justifies the violent anger that spews out of him whenever he doesn't get his own way? *The reason he drinks and his life's in a mess is because his wife left him for his best friend five years ago.* Five years ago? And we think that's a good enough reason why he still hasn't got his act together and moved on? We mistakenly believe that these broken men just happened to be dealt a bad hand by the universe. And we believe we can make it better too. *He needs somebody like me. If he had me to help him, he wouldn't be struggling still. I can heal him.* If you think that, you're more foolish than you realise. And if you don't wake up from this delusion fast, your recycling bin will soon be full up with all the toxic men you keep collecting.

What attracts us to toxic men is our need to feel special. That's our weak spot. That's how needy men hook us on their line. They lavish compliments on us, tell us how good we make them feel, and our kindly but foolish heart is touched by their vulnerability. We are convinced we are the one they have been waiting for all along. If you find yourself continually being drawn into relationships with men who need fixing, it's because you both have negative patterns that dovetail together nicely. Yours is the need to rescue, and his is the need to be a victim. Together, you slot in beautifully like tongue and groove. You need to rescue because it momentarily makes you feel good about yourself. It distracts you from the real issues that are crying out for attention inside you. He sees himself as a victim because it is much easier than taking responsibility for his own actions and behaviour. You will also find that no matter how long you spoon-feed him, he will never grow up. He will always want his mummy to sort things out for him.

A JuicyWoman resists the temptation to fix any man because she knows that he will end up resenting her for emasculating him. She is also aware that she can't relax and surrender into a relationship with a man weaker than herself.

An intelligent woman knows that
addiction and affliction
go hand in hand like
Jack and Jill.
She knows that tumbling down the hill
is not part of self-love.

52

A Man With an Addiction of Any Kind is the Wrong Man

If you date a man with an addiction, you can guarantee that your life will be full of afflictions. You will be dealing with lies and suspicions. You will be coping with hurt and betrayal. You will be worried sick about his welfare and feel helpless at the same time. No matter how sorry you feel for him, don't get involved. No matter how convinced you are that you can help him, you can't. If he hasn't got his troubles sorted out before he meets you, the chances are he won't have afterwards either.

A man who cannot function healthily without his fix, whatever that may be, is a weak man. And a weak man will never be able to earn your respect. Without respect, you won't be able to trust him. If a woman doesn't trust her man, she won't feel secure enough to let go and surrender her heart fully into the relationship. Surrender in this case does not mean giving up your autonomy. It means *leaning into his love* so that he may bring out the best in you. Only when you trust the man can you naturally yield, and when you do, you will flourish and blossom into your loveliness even more. But with a weak man, a woman's juices will only be drained by the mess upon mess that she has to clear up. To rub salt into an already gaping wound, he will invariably end up being resentful, blaming her for his woes because a weak man is incapable of taking responsibility for himself. He thrives on blaming the world for his problems because it is much easier.

Men with drug-related problems will give you all sorts of legitimate reasons why they came to be hooked on the stuff. This is when you want to switch off your sympathetic ear and start listening to your intuitive heart. Whether it's heroin to escape from reality, cocaine to boost confidence in his job, or whisky to help him relax at lunchtime, you must remember that dependency on substance means he can't cope with life as it is. And if he can't cope with life as it is, he certainly won't be able to cope with you as you are. No matter how compelling it is to want to fix his problem, you must avoid doing so at all costs, even if it means not having him in your life. In fact, that would be the most loving decision by far.

These days, with an endless amount of pornographic material available on the internet, it is easy for men to log in and be titillated. But if he spends more time with the computer than with you, you're in trouble. Don't expect him to set you alight with his smouldering kisses or overwhelm you with his deep loving. His sexuality is as deep as your dinner plate. As for a man with sex addiction, no matter how attractive and wonderful his woman is, he will have a tendency to be unfaithful. He is either addicted to the thrill of a new body, the excitement of having forbidden sex, or the buzz of trying out different sexual fantasies with different women. Whatever the reason, such toxic men will only break your heart over and over again.

A man who is hooked on gambling is more than bad news. Not only will you have to contend with his ever-changing moods, depending on whether he wins or loses, but he will also have a nasty habit of betting what he cannot afford to lose. Borrowing money will be his regular thing, and his obsessive interest in your bank account will not amuse you either. With loan sharks as his regular buddies and bailiffs as his sworn enemies, he will also have the habit of telling you he has everything under control. Believe him and you might as well believe that you can live on the moon.

If your date is more interested in competing with your five-year-old nephew on the latest X-Box game than chatting with you, take note. And if he has specially allocated a room in his house for the latest Nintendo Wii, with all the latest gadgets and games, beware. This man is a boy in disguise. He has yet to grow up, and he's not in a hurry to do so either. Unless you are happy for him to spend hours on the joystick rather than making joy with you, stay away from this one. Things will not improve when you live together. They will only get worse. His reality is a virtual one. He won't suddenly be inspired to turn off his machines and spend more time with you. You are much too real for him.

Some of us do seem to attract toxic men in intimate relationships. Often, this is because we have a subconscious need to fix other people's problems. This stems from having low self-esteem, so helping others allows us to feel better about ourselves. Unfortunately, this need to fix is a distraction, and we would do well to focus our loving attention on ourselves. Start to take positive steps towards developing a healthy self-esteem. Seek therapy. Get the help you need to identify why you keep being attracted to men that need fixing. Until you root out the subconscious beliefs that keep driving you towards these toxic men, you will never be free to have a wondrous and happy relationship.

You may also find that you have distorted ideas about love in relationships—that you see neediness as a form of love. Many a woman has stayed in a dysfunctional relationship because she thought she loved the man. Even when the man comes home drunk and uses her as a punch-bag, still she professes her love for him. This is not love. This is lack of love—for herself. Love is never unkind, and love does not inflict pain, on oneself or on another. So when these men declare their undying love for you, know that it can't be love they are talking about. It's not possible for them to know about love as they are not fulfilling the most basic requirement, loving the person they are. This is made evident by the destructive patterns they have towards themselves. What is 'love' to him is actually 'need' in disguise. We must learn to differentiate between the two if we are to have a happy and fulfilling relationship with our man.

A JuicyWoman loves herself too much to be drawn into relationships with toxic men. She understands that these men need professional help and, even if she is highly trained in this domain, it is not her place to sort them out. The most loving thing is to not reinforce his weak behaviour by tolerating it. Then he might just decide to sort himself out because he really wants to be with her.

Man marries woman
and hopes that she doesn't change
- and she does.

Woman marries man
and hopes that he changes
- and he doesn't.

53

You Can Never Change a Man

After you've been with a guy for a few weeks, you start to notice little things about him that you don't approve of. But you're keen to be with him, so you turn a blind eye and tell yourself not to be so finicky. Six to eight months down the line, after the initial *super-tolerant* and *super-nice* stage, these traits start to get on your nerves. But you're convinced he's the one for you, and you find yourself thinking that once you help him to get rid of those 'undesirable' qualities in his personality, you will be perfect together. Stop right there! Don't even think of going down this particular road. It doesn't work.

A smart woman is a woman who knows she can never change a man. She is intelligent enough to realise that what she sees is what she'll get. She's under no illusions that she can change him for the better, even if it is for his own 'good'. She knows that if she doesn't like certain traits in him, she has two alternatives—go somewhere else, or shut up and learn to live with it. It is never an option to change the way a man is. Period.

A smart woman also understands that if the man she's with needs to be different from how he actually is, she's with the wrong man. She knows that unless he is into personal and spiritual growth, which means it is a priority for him to cultivate and expand his understanding of himself and all those around him, it is totally unrealistic to expect his genes to be different to what his parents have given him.

Very often a woman puts up with the wrong man because she believes she can turn him into the right one. She thinks that with her guidance and loving support, or nagging and manipulation, the man will change because he will want to do it for her. Wrong! She doesn't realise one important detail—*that the man is perfectly happy with the way he is, and has no intention of being any different, for her or anyone else.* It is more the case that he wishes the woman would get off his back and leave him alone. This need to change our man is very irritating for him and totally frustrating for us. The sooner we get it into our bright mind that he has every right to be the way he is, that it's none of our business how he conducts himself, and that if we don't like it then we're with the wrong guy, the better! We have no right to insist that another soul should be different to how he is. It doesn't work either. It serves us better to pay attention during the early days and get the following clear in our own mind:

- If he has never been faithful in his previous relationships, don't expect him to be faithful to you.

- If he has never bothered to be close to his children from a previous relationship, don't think that he will win the 'Father of the Year' award when you have kids with him.

- If he is not demonstrative with his feelings, don't expect him to be affectionate towards you or want to sweep you into his arms to comfort you when you're upset.

- If he thinks nothing about crashing out on your sofa whenever he comes round, don't expect him to be Action Man when you start living together. No mild adventures, never mind wild ones, will be on the itinerary.

- If he has commitment phobia, and has never settled down in a long-term relationship, no matter how much he tells you that you're the one he has been waiting for, don't expect him not to do a disappearing act sooner or later.

- If he is a slob, he will remain a slob. He may tidy away the dirty cups and filthy socks in the beginning, but once he feels relaxed and settled he will revert to his old messy ways.

- If he finds your children difficult, he won't suddenly think they are amazing gifts from God and be glad to have them around once you live together. It is more likely he will only find them to be a bone of contention, and you will be piggy in the middle, squashed between resentment and guilt.

- If he has a habit of criticising you and getting mad whenever things don't suit him before you live together, he is not likely to be any different once you are both under the same roof.

Stop thinking: *He's not all that bad, and with my help he'll be better.* If in your eyes he's not good enough as he is, then he's not going to be good enough with your interference. You mustn't get mixed up with parenting a child and being supportive towards your man. One needs your constant guidance and coaching, while the other should only need your feminine love and smiling face.

One common error women make is to live in the *hope* that things will be different in the future. Better to be in the present and see things as they are. It's fairer, and it's more honest too. A man may choose to grow spiritually but it will have to be by his own volition, not because we've cajoled him into doing so. His issues are not our business. Our business is to make sure we go into the relationship with eyes wide open and evaluate things as they are. That way, at least we'll know we haven't created the delusion of a fantasy world that doesn't actually exist.

A JuicyWoman enters into a relationship seeing the man as he is, not how she would like him to be. She is realistic enough not to expect him to change for her, no matter what he says. When the relationship takes a serious turn, the smart question she'll ask herself is: Can I be happy sharing my life with him exactly as he is? If a resounding 'NO' bounces back, she knows to call it quits. If a 'yes' arises out of her calm heart, she is happy to progress it further.

A JuicyWoman knows that any personal issues she has
are simply gateways to her majestic self.
She has no need to broadcast them to her date.
She merely reveals her shining self
once the transformation has taken place.

54

What Disenchants Your Date

Sometimes when we first get together with a man, he seems to be really keen—and then suddenly he drops us for no apparent reason. We can't understand why he is pulling back when not so long ago all seemed hunky dory. Both of you had spent hours enjoying heart-to-heart talks. You told him all about your fears, the unresolved conflicts with your ex, and how you hate your boss. He was so sympathetic and understanding that you couldn't help but reveal all to him. You even told him how much you dislike your plump, voluptuous behind, and he was quick to tell you that he found you sexy. You noticed how reassured you felt, if only for a few seconds. This could be the reason why he has made his quick exit—he knew too much about your warts too soon. Too many home truths have shattered his romantic picture of you, so he's taking his attention elsewhere.

At the start of any relationship, a certain enchantment pervades. We are full of enthusiasm, filled with excitement and packed with hopeful anticipation. He wants to see you as this wonderful woman, sweet smelling and feminine, who brightens his day every time you smile. He loves the way your body moves, like poetry in motion, and he adores the way you flick that cute little fringe each time it shades your gorgeous eyes. He has a natural fascination with the creature you are, and in his fantasy mind, it involves all things beautiful and good. That's why he is enchanted and charmed. If you remember the fairytales, they didn't mention anything about loving warts, at least not at this stage. He is not thinking of the long term—good, solid men usually take much longer than women to decide. He's just enjoying your femininity and all the sweetness you bring when he's in your company.

Now, back to the warts. These days, if you have a wart, you quietly get it 'frozen' until it drops off. You certainly do not announce it to the world. So why should you broadcast your unresolved psycho stuff to anyone who cares to listen, and especially to the one you are trying to enchant? It doesn't make sense.

Telling a man about your problems and personal issues when you're at the early stage of the relationship will disenchant him. It would have a similar effect if he did the same with us. The responsible and empowering way to deal with our personal issues and worries is to get the proper help we need and, here's the important bit, *only from those who have the ability to help us.* Choose to confide in those who can give you good, sensible advice—either professionals who are trained to do the job, or friends who have gone through similar challenges and have emerged shining on the other side. Whatever issues or problems we may have, when we are pro-active and willing to do whatever it requires to get them resolved, they will indeed be resolved. Talking about these deep personal issues with a man before he decides you're the one for him can cast a death sentence over a potential relationship.

No matter how nice he seems, we must remember that he is not here to sort out our internal struggles. If your car breaks down, yes, by all means call him. He will enjoy being the hero and rescuing you before a garage gets the pleasure of receiving your distress signal. Practical help where his muscles can be put to good use is fine. But emotional problems should not be dished onto his plate. No matter how much the man reassures us, it is for us to overcome our inner fears and insecurities. Otherwise, we will only be addicted to the need to be reassured, trapping us in an unhealthy treadmill of neediness. But once we lovingly give ourselves the support to overcome these difficult issues, we will be confident and at ease with the person we are. It is through conquering them that we bring out the extra shine in us. Only then will we be ready to meet life with enthusiasm and joy. Men find such brightness very appealing indeed.

A JuicyWoman realises that personal issues and problems are only opportunities in disguise. They are opportunities to entice the excellence out of us, because we suffer from the delusion of thinking we are less than what we are. She rolls up her sleeves and gets on with sorting them out one by one. And any man who bears witness to such self-empowerment will certainly be enchanted. The knowledge that she will be an emotional asset, as opposed to an emotional liability, is deeply attractive to him. He won't be able to resist her.

≈ ❤ ❤ ❤ ≈

We give a loving service and bury our dead
when their time is over.
It makes sense to do the same
with past relationships.

≈ ❤ ❤ ❤ ≈

55

Bringing Closure to Your Past Relationships

Any unfinished business from a previous relationship leaves behind negativity that will bleed into any new one you try to start. The toxic effect of these unresolved issues will inevitably leak into your new relationship, even if you escape to the other side of the planet. This is because the unfinished business is about you and your own growth, and has nothing to do with the other person, regardless of his actions. No matter where you go, be it a new place or a new relationship, it will always be there, gnawing away inside your head, until you sort it out and lay it to rest once and for all. Even if you and your ex are not on speaking terms, you can still have closure, because without it any new relationship you enter will be tainted by the leftover mess.

How can you tell if you still have unfinished business with your ex?

- If you have the urge to cross the street when you see him coming your way, you do.

- If you find yourself having imaginary arguments with him, then you haven't cut the emotional cords that still bind you together.

- If you find yourself chewing over and over the seeming injustice you endured when you were together, then you have yet to put it to rest.

- If you can't bear to hear nice things being said about him, you have still got him blacklisted. That means you have granted him a special pass to get at you, even if it is just in your own head.

Bringing closure to your old relationships allows you to begin anew.

It allows your wounds to heal and your heart to mend. It gets you out of the gloomy dungeon of resentment and into the cool, crisp air of bright beginnings. Closure allows you to stand in this new ground, arms open wide, head tilted back to soak up the delicious warm sun, breathing in new, loving possibilities as the old cobwebs are being blown away. It also stops your subconscious mind from projecting your ex's past crimes onto the new beloved. All in all, it allows you to have the inner peace that seems to elude many an unforgiving soul.

Yes, *forgiveness* is the ultimate tool for moving on. Do you find forgiving him difficult? Perhaps deep in your subconscious, you believe that if you forgive, it means you are saying it's okay that he did what he did? Perhaps you think if you forgive, it means you condone the awful deed done to you, and that's the same as giving him permission to hurt you again? So not forgiving is a form of self-defence? If these are your beliefs, it's time to hold them up against the light of Love, see how untrue they are and urge yourself towards the healing path.

Forgiveness has nothing to do with the other person. Forgiveness has to do with us, and us alone. In truth, we don't need to be concerned about somebody else's actions. On a spiritual level, we are all accountable for our thoughts and deeds. We do not need to be distressed by the thought that others may 'get away with murder'. On a higher level, no one gets away with anything, no matter how it may look on the surface. There is a natural law of balance and it is always operating with precision, whether we notice it or not. The 'perpetrator' will get his due, the growth opportunity his soul needs, at some point in his evolution. Having this perspective will spin us out of the ugly need to seek revenge. We mustn't stoop low and compromise the noble in us just because we're hurting. Our heart is more magnanimous than that. Generosity is our very nature, and when we pretend otherwise, when we hold back, it hurts.

By letting go of our focus on the other person's 'crime', we can concentrate on releasing ourselves from the suffering caused by holding onto the past. When you forgive, you are literally releasing yourself from the bondage of what is making you unhappy. It is the most loving act we can do for ourselves.

There can be no forgiveness without acceptance. Acceptance in this case means you accept the limitations of his human personality, that people can only be what they are until that is no longer the case. Remembering that we too have our own share of flaws will humble our heart, making it easier for us to accept others for their failings.

Ultimately, there is no one to forgive. If you open your mind wide enough, you will see that all acts and dramas are simply opportunities for us to master the art of Love and be free. We are constantly serving each other through the human drama, a vibrant medium from which we can realise our highest nature. Our enemies are our greatest teachers. They show us what we have yet to heal inside us. Any place we defend is where we're still suffering. And the choice to forgive is a loving decision to end this suffering in us. Love is the only power, and Love is the only way. When you have forgiven him, you can release your ex by using a visualisation technique that will cut any remaining ties that still bind you both in an unhealthy way. It's a simple exercise and will only take a few minutes to do.

Close your eyes and imagine both of you sitting opposite each other in two circles, joined together as if in a figure of 8. Tell him how you feel, with the awareness that he was only doing the best he knew how at that time. When you're ready, say "I forgive you". Now, ask him for forgiveness too, for all the hurt you may have knowingly or unknowingly caused him. After the forgiveness, thank him for all the gifts he has given you in the relationship. Know that everything he has brought to you, be it joy or pain, has served you one way or another in this human journey. Then give him a blessing, wish him well in his life and say "I bless and release you". See yourself holding a pair of golden scissors, cutting across the part where the two circles are joined in the figure of 8, and watch him float away. Repeat this exercise every day until you no longer feel any negative emotions towards him. The thought of him will bother you less and less as time goes by. The evidence of this genuine release is the peaceful feeling you feel within.

To sincerely thank and bless a person whom you believe has caused you hurt is a kind deed towards yourself. It dissolves the anger and resentment that eats away at your peace. Instead of having a part of you trapped in the unpleasant past, it will allow you to be more fully present and enjoy what you have now. It's like having a splinter removed from your finger—there will no longer be a nagging sense of pain that distracts you from concentrating on what is good in the moment. The relief and sense of liberation you feel will take years off your face and bring lightness back into your step. To forgive is an exalted act that immediately returns you to Love's side. Your laughter will be free to join with all the other sweet sounds in the universe.

A JuicyWoman is intelligent enough to know that any ill feeling she has about her ex is to do with her, not him. As an empowered woman, she makes sure she brings her past relationship to closure, cleaning her inner house before the new beloved arrives. She knows the work is not done until she is sure she will have a genuine smile for her ex the next time their paths cross again.

A woman who loves herself
is a woman who will not settle
for just any man.

A woman who loves herself
is a woman who waits patiently
for her beloved to turn up.

56

A Long-term Relationship Suits Our Feminine Soul

Nowadays, women can sustain a comfortable physical life for themselves without a man. We are able to earn good money in what we do, treat ourselves to a nice house and jet off to exotic locations on our own. As portrayed in *Sex and the City*, women are quite capable of having a good time with their girlfriends, having sex with men whenever it suits them, and even having children without needing a man in the house. It seems we can date any man we fancy, chuck him out when he doesn't meet our high standards, find a new one and start all over again. It seems things for women have never been better. We seem to have it all. Or at least on the physical level. But on an emotional level, it's a disaster. Women have never felt more alone and unloved in their lives. Men seem to be confused about what we want from them. The path to eternal happiness seems to have veered off unnoticed while we were busy fighting for equality and competing with them.

The evidence that this particular path is not working too well for us is clear. Frustrating and unsatisfying short-term relationships are like acid to our parched, feminine heart. For those of us who are ready to be deeply loved by a man we trust, ready to be seen in our naked radiance by a man we don't have to impress, it is time for us to try a different path. It is time for us to stop kidding ourselves and see that having short-term relationships does not serve our feminine soul at all. We are cosmically programmed to love forever, to abandon heart and soul to our one true love. Because Love is our nature, all our cells scream to live and die in love, and anything less is a life of torture. If you are single and you profess to not feeling this yearning desire to drown in love, it could be because you are still reeling from a wound that has yet to heal. Your *'I'm happy being single forever'* attitude might be a defence against the fear of further pain.

You have been badly hurt by a man (it doesn't have to be a lover, it could be a father figure) and you are too terrified to trust a man and expose yourself to vulnerability again.

It is vital for us to see that short-term relationships actually drain our feminine essence. Every time a different man comes and goes, our heart bleeds a little. So having bouts of brief encounters is like being bled alive. Eventually our anaemic heart begins to doubt love itself. We begin to form beliefs that say things like, *'love hurts'*, *'relationships are so complicated and difficult'* or *'I'll never meet the right man'*. These beliefs can make us give up on love altogether.

Having short-term relationships also weakens us because every time a man leaves, we feel a little less glorious. We feel as if there is something wrong with us because we haven't managed to find love. And if he doesn't call back when he says he will, we wonder whether we are good enough. Our self-esteem and self-confidence get knocked, and we question if we are desirable. Every time we date a man who is not compatible, we have a little less faith in men. We begin to have a clouded view about the goodness of men, and we let go of the fact that we can be so good for each other.

When we have been hurt a few times, we may choose to stay single as a form of defence. We may even convince ourselves that we don't need a man in our life to be happy. No need for an intimate love in our life? Who are we kidding? We all know that no story is a great story without the dramas of love in it. That's why most women would rather watch a chick flick than a war film. The triumph of human spirit does touch our heart, but nothing overcomes our feminine soul more than the requited love between a man and a woman. Take the love story out of *Titanic* and the movie would not be half as emotionally compelling as it is. Deep down we need our love story to burn brightly in our feminine soul. The Love-being that we are feeds from this inner fire. And only a long-term relationship that is based on trust, Love and joy can ignite this fire.

A JuicyWoman is never casual with relationships. She sees the man she has chosen to be with as a perfect reflection of what she thinks of herself. No matter how tempting it is, no matter how alone she is, she refuses to start relationships with men who are not right for her. She totally and utterly believes in Love and focuses her energies not on looking for the right man, but on preparing herself to be the right woman.

A relationship is the hardest
when you're in it,
to get what you want.

A relationship is the easiest
and sweetest
when you're in it,
to give what you are.

57

The Yoga of Relationships

All women need to be caressed by Love. When we are in Love, we glow brighter than a million suns. We literally light up a room with our radiance when we walk into it. Friends and family comment on how well we look. Happiness is obvious for all to see and partake in. This is because we are born to love and to be ravished in Love. And a long-term relationship allows us to do just that. It is also the safety in which we are blessedly held while being transformed by the fires of life that come in the form of difficulties, challenges and trauma.

It is said that the yoga of relationships is the hardest. To deal with one's own neuroses and unresolved issues is an enormous task by itself. But to have to deal with another person's as well in the same intimate space, and still get along harmoniously with each other, can be a tremendous challenge. But if you are able to crack it and find the formula that works for both of you, then a long-term relationship is also the most rewarding. If you are able to join, live and grow together as a happy unit, not only the two of you reap the rewards of this blessed union, but the world is a better place because of it. The emanation that shines forth from a couple who love and adore each other quietly inspires us to believe in Love. And the gifts and blessings of a good, solid long-term relationship are plenty. It allows you to:

- Have greater resources to ride the challenges of life, because two heads are better than one. Your resources increase not only on a physical level, but on a mental and emotional level too. With the right man, you literally become a greater woman.

- Build love and trust with the same man. Like a flower, we blossom and bloom into our gorgeous radiance under the loving care and trust of a good man.

- Have the relationship as a sacred container in which both individuals are held in Love, while each works through personal limitations and grows to their full potential.

- Share special and deeply meaningful moments with someone who knows you, warts and all, and still adores you.

- Have the opportunity to evolve from neediness to a higher emotional level found in *devotional* Love: a Love that is unconditional and knows know bound.

- Have the unwavering support and deep commitment, through thick and thin, to emerge on the other side a better woman, and he, a better man. You become each other's bedrock from which you weather the stormy times of life.

- Have someone to inspire you, to give you new ideas, and to help you see a more complete picture of whatever you are dealing with.

- Have stability and constancy in your life. This allows you to sink your roots into the depth of who you are, and flourish. The deeper the roots, the higher you reach. Jumping from one short-term relationship to another is a bit like being a plant that is constantly dug up and transplanted; it uses up all its energy adapting to a new environment, rather than being able to focus on growth.

- Provide a stable environment in which your children (if you have any) can grow and develop. This, in turn, helps them to develop the skills and understanding needed to live and function in a harmonious way with the opposite sex.

Steady love and constant affection from the same person has a quality that *builds*, as opposed to the draining quality of brief relationships. Unseen to the eye, it is an invisible strength that is tangible to the heart. It is this strength that makes us more aerodynamic when encountering the winds of change in our life. The benefits and blessings of being in a long-term relationship are countless indeed.

While a man may be able to exist quite happily, feeding on his success and achievements in life, a woman needs Love to nourish her heart, no matter how successful she is in her work life. Love is the food that feeds and nurtures our feminine heart. It is not the case that we are waiting to be given this Love by a man. That is the kind of erroneous thinking that turns us into needy creatures and strips us of our feminine glory. We are not waiting to be given Love in a relationship. Instead, being in a relationship allows us give the Love we are. The whole dance and purpose of life is simply Love giving itself back to itself. The more we give, the more Love we will expand in our reality, and the more we will experience it in our everyday life.

Relationships fail when people enter into them in order to take from them. And we do that when we don't realise our inner treasures, the fullness of our Love nature. We become emotional paupers and believe it is the man's job to give us what we want, to make us happy. Of course this distorted approach doesn't work. Anything that contradicts our true nature can never work because it has no integrity.

Who we are is a creature of Love. We are born *to love*, not born *to be loved*. Being loved is simply the sweet, natural consequence that comes from being who we are—a being of Love. And if you have forgotten this truth, then you must direct all your energy into awakening yourself from this nightmare. There are so many good spiritual and self-help books out there. Read the lot, and read some more. Join study groups that are focused on growth and personal development. Sit and learn with enlightened teachers. Have friends around you who are more spiritually advanced than you are—they will take you further. The more you realise what an incredible being you are, and how huge your loving heart is, the more success you will have in the yoga of relationships. You will be adored. Because you always receive what you give away.

A JuicyWoman appreciates all the beautiful gifts a long-term relationship brings. She sees how it gives her untold opportunities to shine forth the beauty of her loving heart. She also sees that a good relationship can be the holy vessel that helps the man and woman burn up any make-believe inadequacies they may have, allowing both to rise to their great noble height as individuals, and as a beautiful unit.

❧ ❤ ❤ ❤ ❧

What makes a woman fascinating
is the immense depth her heart can love
and the unlimited height her spirit can soar.

❧ ❤ ❤ ❤ ❧

58

Be a Fascinating Woman

No matter how long a woman has been with her man, she loves it when he notices the little things: the way she's wearing her hair differently, the scent of her new perfume, or how pretty she looks in her new summer dress. We love it when he looks up from whatever he's doing and gives us a sweet compliment. It makes us feel feminine and attractive. Our heart glows when he gives us one of his special looks, a look that says, *"I think you're wonderful and I'm so glad to have you in my life"*. It doesn't matter if we've been with him for twenty months or twenty years, each time he affirms his love by giving us this intimate attention, we fall in love with Love again. Yet it's common to see couples sitting at restaurant tables and looking everywhere but at each other. What happened there? Is there anything women can do to stop such a fate befalling them?

One of the things that keeps your man fascinated is a sense of mystery, of not knowing everything about you. Applying the 'keep-him-wondering' technique every now and then is good. Don't let him think that he knows exactly how you will behave or react with him. Even after ten years of living together, you can still surprise him from time to time with the way you respond to him. Jump on him and give him a full, hearty bear hug when he comes home from work. At other times, have the table beautifully laid, complete with candles, a nice bottle of wine and a delicious Moroccan meal or something you don't usually have. The key here is to be creative. This is not about him; it's about you. This is about you broadening your inner horizons, sampling new things for the sake of self-discovery. If you have never done this before, it may unnerve him a little in the beginning, but that's not a bad thing. It will keep him on his toes and prevent him from switching off his attention for you completely. It makes him aware that he doesn't know everything about you. And that keeps him nicely on your scent.

What desensitises your man and makes him switch off his attention for you is predictability. Nagging away at him is a definite no-no. Or telling him every worry and concern you have in your head. Don't use him as a sounding board for all your problems, either. While you may want to discuss major things that affect your life together, it is better to work quietly with your own little doubts and fears and overcome them yourself. Many women rely on their man for the feelgood factor, or for reassurance when they are plagued by self-doubt. This is your inner work, and it has nothing to do with him. Until you have overcome your inner monsters, nothing anyone says will really make them go away anyway, so you might as well get on and deal with them for good.

A woman who doesn't know what she wants, but spends her life giving people what she thinks they want, doesn't fascinate her man, because there's nothing fascinating about resentful martyrs. And neither does a woman who doesn't know what makes her happy but runs around after others all day thinking it makes them happy. Such a woman doesn't know who she is, what makes her heart sing, or what her soul needs. This syndrome is common after many years of being married, bringing up children and looking after everyone around her but herself.

In order to fascinate, we have to be *interesting*. This means having interests, activities or hobbies outside the relationship or family. Doing things that you enjoy makes you feel good about yourself. Take a class. Develop a hobby. Meet people. Each individual you meet brings something to your spirit and enriches you in ways you may not even be aware of. Every experience you have expands your mind and opens your heart, if you let it. Keep learning, keep growing. Go beyond your little patch and make room in your consciousness for everything and everyone. From time to time, ponder on the stars out there in the dark night, twinkling and winking at you in delight. Awe your mind with thoughts about infinity and the perfection of nature. Investigate deeply into life and all its wondrous mysteries. Treasures are never found on the surface, but in wondrous depths. We are only as interesting to others as the breadth and depth of our own interests.

The deeper you go, the more passionate you become. Passion is the fire that ignites your heart for active living. It makes the heart love more fully. Passion also becomes fuel for your boldness. A bold heart, a heart that is not afraid to go against the tide, is very attractive and captivating at the same time.

A JuicyWoman will always plough her own furrow. Self-possessed and intelligent, she thinks for herself, has her own ideas and stands up for her values. Languishing in comfort zones is not her style, and she goes out of her way to try new experiences. She meets any fear that might crop up with boldness. Being passionate makes her a deep-sea diver of life, and she never stops being fascinated by it, making her a fascinating creature to her man.

An enchantress is a woman
who knows what makes her heart sing.

An enchantress is a woman
who knows how to make other hearts sing.

59

You Are an Enchantress

If you want to get the best out of your man, don't tell him what to do. Enchant him instead. When your man is enchanted by you, he will do anything to please you. He will want to make you happy because when you are, so is he. Having a happy woman next to him is a great compliment, and it makes him feel a success. This good feeling in him will reverberate in all areas of your life and bless everything in its path.

How do you enchant your man? By making sure that each time he walks through the door, you are delighted to see him, no matter what. Your delight must be genuine because faking it won't do. Perhaps you can't see why you should be elated for no apparent reason. Well, he came home to you, didn't he? You can start by taking that as a compliment. Jump on him and wrap your gorgeous body and soul around him. He may think you've gone mad, but he will absolutely love the attention.

Enchanting your man means making him feel he's the best in the world. As they say, a man's ego needs to be stroked. Well, there is much to be said for making him feel the most important and wonderful man to you. Such behaviour encourages him to do his very best. He wants to be seen as the king in your eyes. And if you want to be treated like a queen, that's what you need to do; you must always give what you want to receive.

Your beloved should also be your hero. Each time he does a little thing for you, tell him how great he is. Let him see your appreciation by the joy on your face. No sane man can resist being charmed by his woman when she is radiant and bright. Smiles from you work wonders for his heart and well-being. Don't struggle to drag the heavy vacuum cleaner up the stairs. Banging it all the way up those steps will not earn you extra brownie points. Instead, be feminine. Tell him how strong he is as he hoists the appliance up the stairs with hardly any effort. The idea here is not to pretend to be a sycophant, but to find authentic ways to enjoy his masculinity. If you want him to treat you like a princess, then you must *wholeheartedly* embrace him as your knight. Then, and only then, will he be glad to sweep you up into his arms as you are about to walk through wet grass, if only to stop your lovely shoes from getting soaked.

Never ask. Always request. And when he has done what you wanted, always thank him from the bottom of your gracious heart. We usually reserve such generosity for friends and acquaintances. Our man deserves it more than any other. For choosing us to be his woman, for loving us regardless, and for being here for us, he deserves the best treatment from us all the time. Okay, realistically speaking that might not be possible, but at least with the ever-present intent to treat him well, we stand a better chance of giving him more of a sweet time.

It is women who usually instigate the divorce in a marriage. As a general rule, we do so when we no longer feel loved and adored in the relationship, or he has taken his attention somewhere else. What part do we play in this disenchantment process? We are usually acutely aware of how he no longer makes us feel special or beautiful. But are we just as aware of how we consistently turn him away from us with our own behaviour towards him? By nagging him? By making him feel that no matter what he does, it's never good enough? By criticising him whenever he does something his way and not ours? We treat him as if he owes us our happiness. We remain unmindful of how we sour his tender feelings towards us when we become un-feminine in our approach towards him. We even believe that our unloving behaviour is for his benefit!

There are only two routes a man can take when we interact with him: towards us or away from us. So before you act, react or respond, keep in mind which direction you want him to take. This awareness will help you choose actions that will nurture the relationship rather than destroy it. Our actions are completely powerful in determining the outcome of the moment. We don't have to be concerned about his behaviour. We just need to be unwavering in our positive manner towards him. Have faith in the good. Your goodness and integrity will sweetly draw the best out of him. Your openness and softness towards him will captivate his heart and attention. It's the all-powerful, feminine way.

A JuicyWoman knows it is her divine feminine right to be an enchantress. The enchantment door is always within her reach as she constantly affirms how wonderful and great her man is. She is aware that how she loves and honours him will determine if he is heartfully present or emotionally absent in the relationship. She endeavours to be so irresistible that he just can't keep away.

When you know who you are,
what exudes from your being
is like nectar to the bees.
You cause those around you
to produce such sweetness.

60

Only Say What is Sweet to the Ear

The amount of time that we have in a day with our man is limited. By the time both of you are back home and ready to sit down and have quality moments together—away from work, away from chores and away from children—there are not many hours left. We actually spend more time with our colleagues than we do with our partner! Yet, instead of using every single minute of what's left to enjoy each other's company, and celebrate the love you have together, you unwittingly push him away. Behaviour such as nagging, moaning and complaining does just that. A great spiritual teacher once said, *"Only speak what is sweet to your tongue and sweet to the ear of your listener."* If we endeavour to only say kind and loving words to our man, he has no option but to love us in the dearest of ways.

When someone communicates to you in a soft, loving manner, even if it is something that you are not keen to hear, you know it is much easier to take it on board because you don't feel threatened or attacked. The same rule applies to him. If your way of communicating is one of attack, he will only feel defensive and automatically shut you out. It is then almost impossible to get him to see your point of view. And if your general trend is to criticise or moan at him, his affection and adoration towards you will eventually evaporate away into nothing. Without adoration in his heart, he is less likely to want to find a thousand ways to make you happy. And why should he? Would you be motivated to treat someone well if she constantly made you feel you were not good enough? Quite the opposite! You would be more inclined to want to stay away, to work overtime because colleagues are more pleasant to you, or to hang out with your mates at the pub because at least you can have a laugh with them. Some men choose to go out and play golf, or some other sport, just to get some peace and quiet.

Perhaps right now you are mentally arguing that he criticises you too. That he too makes you feel less than perfect. And that he undermines your confidence by constantly highlighting your mistakes. Instead of appreciating the hours you have spent trying to cook a new dish for him, he steamrollers your confidence by saying, "Yuk, I don't like it." All you can hear is a shattering sound as your hopes of being the new Nigella Lawson are dashed into a thousand tiny pieces. And so, in your defence, you tell him a few home truths about his own inadequacies. In your frustration and hurt, you compare him with David next door, who has just bought his wife a new car and is taking the whole family to Mauritius for a five-star holiday. With one ungracious swoop, you reduce his male self-esteem to the size of a pea.

What you have here is a stalemate situation. By criticising each other and grabbing any opportunity you can to have a go at each other, neither of you wins. Instead, you both lose—heavily. You lose trust in each other, you lose your comradeship in the relationship and, most of all, you lose intimacy with each other.

If you are both in the destructive pattern of criticising each other, then one of you must make what looks like a sacrifice, and be the first one to break the chain of negative behaviour. You might think, "Why should I be first to make the changes? He might take advantage." Not if you understand the law of love. Love begets love. If you want to feel loved and be adored, then willingly be the first one to make steps towards it. It is an intelligent thing to do. When we are the first to give up our warfare, far from being a sacrifice, it is actually a mark of generosity in our soul, to be able to put aside pride (which has no real significance in spiritual terms anyway) and do what is necessary to restore beauty and harmony in our life.

Someone who came to me for relationship advice told me that she and her husband had got into this vicious circle of criticising each other. She felt she was criticising him out of defence. Whenever he pointed out to her what seemed like a failing, she would quickly react by giving examples that he wasn't perfect either. He also felt neglected by her as she was either preoccupied with their three young kids or giving foot massages to her friends. I asked her if she wanted to be loved, adored and worshipped by her husband. She nodded without hesitation, so I said, "This is what you must do. From now on, make him the most important thing on your list of priorities. When he comes home from work, make sure the table is laid and candles lit, even if you haven't started cooking yet. This lets him know that a nice meal is on the way. It shows that you have considered him and appreciate the fact that he is working hard to keep the bank manager happy. Make sure you smell sweet and meet him at the door with your gorgeous, smiling face. And make sure you massage his feet first before you massage anyone else's. For taking care of you and his family, he deserves that priority." I saw her three days later at a local store. She said she had done as I had advised, and that she couldn't believe the drastic change in her husband's behaviour. Over the weekend, they had been at a dinner dance, and he had not stopped dancing with her. It had never happened before in the seven years they had been together. He even said that whereas before he had loved her sixty percent, now he loved her one hundred percent! She thought I had performed a miracle by helping her achieve such instant and wonderful results with her husband. I clarified that it is actually *love* that performs the miracle.

A JuicyWoman knows that whatever she does or says to her man, she is either encouraging him to draw her closer or causing him to push her away. She finds that when she makes a point of living from her love centre, it is easy for sweet and loving words to flow from her lips. Communication becomes a constant practice as she continues to master the art of Love.

A JuicyWoman is a woman whose presence
brings the best out of a person
without her uttering a single word.

ê❤❤❤ê

61

Is Coming Home to You An Irresistible Option?

Is coming home to you such an attractive and inviting option that your man simply cannot refuse? If you ask yourself that question, you will either hear a resounding 'YES!' or a sheepish 'No'. Every time you see your man, do you make him feel manly and master of his own universe? Or do you emasculate him by focussing on what is wrong with him or the relationship? Do you find yourself going on and on like a jumping record, complaining that he is:

- Spending too much time at work
- Spending too much time with his friends
- Spending too much time on the computer
- Spending too much time in front of the TV
- Spending too much time with everyone else except you
- Being constantly late for dinner
- Being too lazy to pull his weight around the house
- Being deaf or too disinterested to listen to what you are saying
- Being too tired to help with the children
- Add your own here...

If you find yourself saying 'yes' to many of the statements above, then he is coming home to you because he feels he has to, rather than because he can't keep away.

How do you make coming home to you an irresistible option? Yes, believe it or not, how much time he spends with you is an *option* for him. You may like to think of it as a responsibility, but it's not. Staying married or committed to you is a chosen responsibility, but how much quality time he actually spends with you is an option that he exercises. That is why many men are able to legitimately stay away from their women under the pretext of work or other reasons like hobbies and sports. This is not to say that a man shouldn't have his leisure pursuits. Of course it is healthy for both parties to have their own interests. We are referring here to relationship patterns where, rather than having a heart-to-heart bond with each other, the man and woman simply exist under the same roof. To such couples, the relationship has become a convenience rather than a celebration of love.

Now that we have established that wanting to spend time with you is an option for him, how do you make it such a pleasant experience that he will want to hurry home to you every night?

No matter what you are doing, the moment you hear him come through the front door, drop everything and rush to give him the most exuberant greeting from the bottom of your generous heart. *Nothing pleases a man more than to see his woman feeling excited and happy to see him. And when your man is pleased, his natural urge is to make you happy too.*

When he comes through the door, look gorgeous and sweet-smelling, like those lovely fresh flowers you adorn your house with. *A man delights in enjoying his woman's femininity. The more feminine his woman is, the more he wants to protect, love and cherish her.*

If you don't have anything nice to say to him, don't say anything at all.
Tell him a million times a day how much you love him.
When he does something for you, no matter how mundane, no matter how small, tell him how wonderful he is.
Tell him he is your hero when he carries the heavy shopping bags.
Thank him whenever he helps you out.

Never criticise him in front of others.
Criticising him in the presence of his family or friends wounds his masculine heart.
It emasculates him and he won't feel tender towards you.
Speak only good about him, be it in his presence or behind his back. This attitude not only creates a loving synergy in your relationship, but it will also help you to stay in love with him. Focussing on the positive reminds you why you fell in love with him in the first place.

Appreciation carries an invisible power that makes a person want to give more. Appreciation engenders not only generosity, but it also expands the love that is already there. It is easy to appreciate him if you don't take him for granted. Each time you compliment him, you are putting a good investment into the emotional bank so that there will be plenty to draw upon when both of you have an emotional 'rainy day'. If you have to discuss a difficult issue with him, you can temper your language by not projecting blame on him. Take responsibility for your own feelings and be open. Don't be afraid to be vulnerable too. There is no need to use attack language. A man who has a soft spot for his woman will always want to know what is upsetting her. He will want to make it better for her if he can, because that's what love does.

When you are kind and loving towards him, you naturally feel good about yourself too, because you are being true to your Love-self. Your confidence in the relationship rises, and because you both treat each other well, the relationship goes from strength to strength. It becomes something quite beautiful, precious and rare, and it nourishes your feminine heart. As you radiate the Love that you are, and make it such a sweet experience for him to come home to, he will always be eager to be there to cast his loving eyes upon your beautiful face.

A JuicyWoman does not take her relationship with her beloved for granted, no matter how long they have been together. She takes each day as a compliment that he has chosen to be with her for that day. This radical outlook allows her attitude towards the relationship to stay fresh and alive. She is never complacent when it comes to Love. She knows that the power to enchant or destroy an intimate relationship ultimately lies in the hands of the woman.

❧ ❤ ❤ ❤ ❧

A woman who is switched on
by her passion
and deep spirituality
has no problem
getting her man's loving attention.

❧ ❤ ❤ ❤ ❧

62

Exaggerate and Magnify Your Feelings Towards Him

How often are you frustrated by your man's seeming insensitivity and obliviousness to how you are feeling? Does it puzzle you that while your girlfriends have no problem reading your moods and emotional fluctuations, your man seems to be clueless as to what is going on for you? You end up interpreting his ignorance as not caring, his inattentiveness as a lack of interest in you. You couldn't be further from the truth. Unless your relationship has soured to a point where you both only feel resentment and anger towards each other, you can be certain that your man cares deeply whether you are happy or sad. Your emotional disposition matters a lot more to him than you think. Most men tend to get his identity and purpose in life through work, but being able to make his woman happy gives him the fulfilment of being successful as her lover and beloved. It also nurtures the protector in him, whose fundamental drive is to look after and protect those close to him. Every man lives to see his woman happy. Seeing her happy makes him happy, and it brings a deep satisfaction to his heart.

Unlike men, we women are far more aware of our environment, and especially of the moods and feelings of people around us. We need this kind of attentiveness to care for our young ones, and to ensure that their physical and emotional needs are met. The feminine force of life is energy (*shakti* in yoga terms), and movement is its expression. So as females, we experience the fullness of this energy movement much more than our male counterparts. Emotions are 'energies-in-motion', and given the fact that we women tend to operate from our emotional centre, whether we like it or not (while men tend to get stuck in their head), we naturally experience the fullness of this energy and movement a lot more than men. Movement is our natural way, which explains why there are usually more women than men on the dancefloor. It is healing and therapeutic for women to dance. And it is our inherent nature to always be the more emotional one. With energy and emotions being part of our intrinsic make-up, we are always aware of how others are feeling, and we will automatically pick up any fluctuation in the moods of others.

However, the creature you are and the creature your man is are poles apart. Nature has designed men to do a different job from us. Back in the caveman days, men would spend hours or even days totally focussed on stalking and killing their prey so that they could feed the tribe. Our modern men still have the same drive and instincts. Most men are completely goal-oriented. To get the job done is a top priority for the male mind. In general, men find it easier to be unemotional and impersonal in business, so much so that they can work closely and cooperate with someone they utterly dislike, just to achieve the results needed. We would find that challenging because women are process-oriented rather than goal-oriented. Being process-oriented means that what we experience moment by moment is extremely important to us, as we are deeply affected by the process itself. As women, although we care about the outcome, we are just as concerned about the feelings of everyone involved, including our own. It is easier for men to ignore the emotional side of things, while it is almost impossible for us to do so.

Being naturally more focussed also means that, from time to time, your man is unaware of what is going on for you. Because he is goal-oriented and he cares strongly about success, he can often be lost in his own agenda, be it work or the fortunes of his football team. And as the masculine is not as sensitive to the energy environment as we are, he can't feel the subtle energetic messages you are giving him until your energy is quite loud. You could be upset for days before he notices and asks, *"Is there something wrong?"* Our man needs us to be overt when it comes to communicating our feelings to him.

When he has done something nice for you, make it obvious that you are thrilled by it. Let your face express your delight and let your body openly come alive with what you are feeling. Soften your body and let the joy flow through. We are so beautiful and feminine when we move with our gladness.

That's what femininity is all about—flowing beauty. Our feminine flow naturally enchants his masculinity, which is more controlled and stoic by nature. His masculine essence is visually and energetically enhanced by the animation and pleasure shown in our physical form. If you are pleased to see him when he comes home, jump on him, wrap your gorgeous legs around him and plant a Juicy kiss on him. Such spontaneity and carefree attitude in the way you express yourself makes a man feel vibrant and alive. He will love you for it. When you are happy, make it obvious. Let this positive emotion flood your whole body. Let your face beam with happiness, your voice lilt with delight. The more you *magnify* your positive feelings by giving the fullest of expression to them in the sounds and movements you make, the more joyous you will feel. And the more enlivened he will be. Men love it when we amplify our delight. Literally dance with joy. You may not feel comfortable doing that in public, but in your private moments, don't compromise your delight. Your aliveness, flow and vibrancy are your unique gifts to your man. It invigorates and energises him.

The same goes when your man is off the mark, when his integrity is being compromised by hollow pursuits and narrow-mindedness. Let him know just as loudly. Show your disgust with all the proficiency of an award-winning actress. Don't hold back your tone or body language. As with your pleasure, magnify your displeasure as well, and your man will notice.

If he has said something that hurts, rather than withdrawing from him and shutting your wounded self away for hours on end, just recoil and say, "Ouch!" He will notice immediately and ask you what is wrong. You can then tell him that you are upset by what he has said or done. Convey to him your vulnerability without blaming him. In the moment when he has hurt you, *show* it, rather than talking to him about it after you've been brooding about it for hours. Otherwise, the primary feeling of hurt will be reinforced by the secondary emotion of built-up anger, and it will come out all wrong and accusing. In other words, show him hurt, not blame. Let him know the instant he has hurt your feelings. It is much healthier and kinder to you both, and to the relationship. Keeping a long list that dates back several decades won't help him to understand the point you are making now. It won't help your sanity either.

The more explicit your feelings are, the more you will grab his attention. Of course, we are talking about being authentic here rather than being neurotic. It is no good being a predictable drama queen, screaming at him like a demented banshee, throwing crockery at him and then expecting him to want to listen to you. If you do that, he will tune you out. That is not going to get you what you want; you will only have more of what you don't want—a disinterested man who would rather do something else instead of giving you his attention and love. But on those occasions when he may have genuinely hurt you and may not have realised that he has done so, show him the pain in your eyes and disbelief in your body. Make it blatantly obvious in that moment. Reflect to him what he has done in your movement rather than give him a lecture. To a man, actions are definitely louder than words. We tend to say too much and not show enough. Bottling it up and not saying anything when he has hurt your feelings is not constructive either. When you don't reflect to your man that he is hurting you, you are unwittingly training him to carry on hurting you. And he wouldn't have a clue that is what he is doing. He would be totally surprised when, years later, you rattle off a list that's longer than both your arms put together, of his dismeanours and unholy actions towards you. It is our responsibility to take care of our feelings and help our man understand where he has gone wrong. To do so without prejudice is a useful skill we can all master. This effort will be rewarded by a relationship that is joyously honest, sweetly loving and deeply intimate.

A JuicyWoman is aware of how she enlivens her man whenever she magnifies her delight at something he has done for her. Thrill, excitement, joyousness, elation and enthusiasm, all of these are her natural domains, and she does not hold back in expressing them. Her body exudes liveliness and pleasure, easily captivating her man's attention. He can tell straight away when she is not happy. And he will want to make it right because nothing gives him more pleasure than to see her smiling again.

እ. ❤ ❤ ❤ እ.

Yielding into the soft folds of Love
is a divine experience
that every woman can have.

እ. ❤ ❤ ❤ እ.

63

To Be Truly Loved, You Must Surrender into His Love

Unless she has sexual leanings towards someone of the same gender, every woman on this planet wants to be absolutely adored, unashamedly worshipped and gloriously loved by her man. And, in turn, she will lavishly love and hero-worship him into sweet, sweet, bliss. That is the ideal picture. It is sad to say, but in reality most women feel they are a million miles away from this blissful situation. Many are disillusioned with intimate relationships, while most don't believe such a heavenly state can exist in real life. So we stop making the effort, not believing things can improve. We turn our heart away from the relationship and indulge ourselves with chocolates and concentrate on romantic movies instead, temporarily quenching our parched heart with some fantasy story. But it is just a quick fix. Deep down, we may still unconsciously dream about moonlit walks by the riverbank with 'the one'. But all this time he could have been sleeping in the same bed as us, eating at the same table and living in the same house, yet we have not recognised him! How can this be? How is it possible that this longed-for beloved has been right before our very eyes for so long and we have failed to identify him?

The need to control is the issue here. When we don't trust our man, we automatically try to take charge, and not only control the situation, but to rule him as well. This unfeminine behaviour turns him from the dashing prince he actually is into a frog! We have no idea how much power we yield in shaping the reality around us. Through ignorance, we rob ourselves of a wonderful relationship. Instead of trying to control the man (unless he's a wimp, he will resent you for it anyway), we would fare better in our quest to achieve what our tender heart longs for by surrendering into his love. How do we do that? First of all, by relinquishing the need to wear the trousers in the relationship—it de-feminises you and robs both you and him of your soft, sweet, feminine self. Every time you tell him what to do and how he should handle his affairs, you emasculate him. Every time you emasculate him, you respect him a little less. Every time your respect for him wanes a little, so does your trust. Without trust, there is no way you will be able to relax into the relationship and experience the depth of his love for you.

Every love story that captures our imagination has a handsome hero who sweeps the beautiful heroine off her feet. He carries her to a place, be it emotional or physical, that she otherwise would not have got to by herself. A love story that depicts the heroine dominating her man and bossing him around will never enchant our feminine heart. Our soft feminine wants to yield into the strong masculine. So if we want a relationship that fulfils us on the deepest level, we must learn to step back and let our man take control of himself and his life; it is the only way he will become a master of his own destiny. Controlling your man will only train him to be dependent on you, which is like having an additional child in the family. Eventually you will feel exhausted and lonely because you are doing it all by yourself. You will resent that, while he resents you.

We need to watch out for the *'I'm only trying to help'* mindset. This is usually another guise that we use to assume control. We take on an air of superiority and, thinking that we know better than him, tell him where to park the car, when to ask his boss for a raise, or how to look after the children when we have left them in his care. All these so-called 'helpful' gestures are simply loud statements that say, *"I know better than you do"* and *"I don't trust you to do a good job"*, which basically translates as *"I don't think you are good enough!"* This certainly won't bring out the best in him. You turn him into a defensive creature who wastes his energy trying to justify why he's doing what he's doing, when he could be spending every ounce of it loving you! That's not smart.

There is a great difference between letting your man know what you would like, and telling him what to do. When you enlighten him about your preferences, he gets to maintain his masculine integrity and also has a chance to please you, which every man who loves his woman enjoys doing. When you tell him what to do, you emasculate him, and that gets his hackles up and tends to make him dig his heels in further. In treating him like a kid, you're being his mother, and in that instant, you become less attractive to him. No healthy man fancies his mother.

Surrendering to your man's love means you don't scheme, manipulate or bully him to get your own way. A man whose masculine integrity is intact and knows that he is being respected and loved by his woman would want her to have her own way anyway. Nothing rocks a man's world as much as seeing his woman deliriously happy.

To surrender is to *yield*. And you can only yield if you trust and have faith in him. When you see his strength and capabilities, so will he. When you only see his weaknesses and doubts, so will he. This is the blessing or curse you bestow upon him as his woman. To practise noticing and, more importantly, *highlighting* his good qualities, while ignoring the lesser ones, will help bring those wondrous virtues to the forefront even more. This is one of the greatest gifts you can give him.

Honour the decisions he makes, even if your ideas are different. Do not squash or belittle his ideas. Listen to what he says with genuine interest. It will help you get to know your man deeper. Stop those disapproving looks and eye-rolling gestures. They only serve to make you look unattractive to him. Instead, respect the man you are with by listening to him. Respect has this awesome power of breeding intimacy in a relationship.

If necessary, change the way you communicate with your beloved. It is not what we say but how we say it that matters. As a golden rule, don't talk to him in a manner that you would not use with your best friend. If there's something you would like him to do, request sweetly, rather than asking or demanding that he should comply. A good mental attitude that stops you from being complacent and taking him for granted is to tell yourself that he's with you because he *wants* to be. Feel the compliment in your heart. You don't own him, and he does not owe you. That means everything he offers you is a gift. You have the right to receive his gifts but no right to demand what he does not offer. Being married for a long time still does not warrant such rights either! The sooner we see our intimate relationship as a privilege, the quicker we will get to witness our ecstatic happiness. The more grateful we are, the more we shall have. This law of gratitude lavishly indulges all those who are wise enough to practise its dictat.

What is the cost of not surrendering into your man's loving? You will be a tired, tense, resentful and busy woman. The need to be in control, to chase after every detail, means you have less time to relax, less chance to be happy, and less opportunity to enjoy yourself. You won't get to experience the bliss and the joy of being 'carried': by his strong loving arms, or by the sweet current of being an adored and deeply loved woman.

There are times or conditions when a woman must not surrender. You must not surrender and yield to a man who is abusive, be it physically, mentally or emotionally. If he is a bully then the most loving thing you can do is to get the hell out of there. Neither should you surrender to a man who has addiction problems. Or if he is not capable of being loyal and faithful to you. The most healing thing you can do is to dive deep into yourself and enquire with honesty why you need to be with such men. Find out what the pay-offs are, sort out your emotional baggage and take a more loving attitude towards yourself. Seek counsel from wise friends or professionals to sort out this unhealthy pattern. Every woman deserves to be happy and have a wonderful relationship. She only needs to be willing to take the right steps towards it.

When you surrender into your man's loving, you affirm him. It strengthens him and reinforces the confidence in him. You have a strong, powerful man to trust and yield into. This turns him on and, in return, he lights your fire. You feel more alive in your femininity and he becomes that sexy man who appeals to you. Your relationship will be drenched in sweet tender moments, which is just what your womanly heart longs for. You get the chance to be your best self, the fully gorgeous, sensual and loving creature that you are meant to be. The man you fell in love with can return to you, and be that perfect man you have always wanted him to be. He is your hero because you trust and respect him, and he will take you further than you can take yourself. Your love together will open both of you up to tender places neither of you have ever been to before. This is exactly the kind of love and relationship a woman lives for. A friend of mine who has been married for twenty years and recently learnt to surrender to her husband's loving said: "How funny that I've spent my whole marriage trying to change him into the man of my dreams, and then when I make the conscious effort to stop all of that, he instantly becomes even more fantastic and lovelier than the man I wanted him to be!!!"

A JuicyWoman is a woman surrendered to Love. It is her feminine strength to yield into the potency and vigour of the masculine in her man. When both are joined in harmony, infinite possibilities are born in the relationship. By letting go of control, manipulation and emotional bullying towards her man, she naturally earns the privilege of his deep loving. Intimacy and passion become the holy threads that weave both their loving hearts together.

A gracious woman is a woman who feels
a million dollars
and makes others feel no less.

64

Flirt With Your Man –
Before Someone Else Does

Do you flirt with your man? *"Of course not!"* you may exclaim. *"We've been together far **too long** to be flirting any more"*. That's erroneous thinking. Here is why you must flirt with him.

- Flirting with your beloved is a must if you want to feel sensuous and feminine in your own womanly skin.

- Flirting with your man is a must if you want your relationship to thrive on intimacy, passion and aliveness.

- Flirting with your partner is a must if you want to keep other unethical women's hands off him.

At the beginning of a relationship, we flirt to capture his attention and lure him into our world. Our feminine charms are on full blast. We compromise nothing as we enchant, thrill and tease him until he succumbs to our bewitching ways. Our lips utter all the right words, while our gorgeous body responds beautifully to his exquisite touch. Our eyes shine with delight whenever we see him. Then we bag our man and an invisible force seems to appear out of nowhere and flick that Juicy switch off! We are now normal and mundane. Having the man as a permanent fixture seems to have landed us on a different planet, where excitement, vivacious merriment and sweet pleasure seem to live in exile. Planet Humdrum.

Flirting with your man should continue to be a way of life, no matter how long you've been together. It makes you more aware of your feminine self, as opposed to just being the co-provider, housekeeper, cook, mother, wife and all the other roles our noble female heart plays. You get to experience your soft feminine qualities rather than the usual self-attack criticisms that roll around in your head. You feel more attractive as a woman too. Flirting with your man helps you to unlock the tender and fragrant aspect of being a woman. As you become more in touch with your femininity, you also become more aware of your man's masculine essence. These essences polarise each other in a beautiful way, bringing out the tender, playful side in both of you. You enjoy being a woman while he enjoys being your man.

While he is at work, spice things up a bit for him by sending him a flirty text – *'Thinking of you while I was in the hot, steamy shower this morning...'* Be creative. Start flexing those long-forgotten flirtatious muscles. Leave saucy messages in his email from time to time. You can be as subtle or as explicit as you want. When you are out together in public, find a secret moment and touch him in an intimate way. Let him do the same to you. Having your man surreptitiously pinch your lovely bottom while no one's looking creates an intimate, playful bond between the two of you. As a committed couple, the more you behave in an enticing and loving manner with each other, the more bonding your relationship will be and the more secure you will feel within it.

Regular flirting is essential for couples in a long-term relationship. It makes both the man and woman feel attractive and desirable. If your interaction with your man is only about practical matters, when a flirtatious female comes along and takes a liking to him, he could be vulnerable to her attention. Just as flirting makes you feel feminine and attractive, it has a similar effect on your man too. If you've never given him this kind of personal attention, when he suddenly gets it from an attractive female, it is difficult for him not to be seduced by the enlivening feeling he's getting. He needs to feel he is more than just a money-generating machine for paying household bills and providing for the family. Perhaps many an affair could have been avoided if the wife had paid her husband more compliments and lavished her flirtatious attention on him. Personal attention somehow makes both the man and woman feel more secure in the relationship.

A JuicyWoman knows that one of the basic principles of life is that nature abhors a vacuum; if you don't make your man feel special, one day somebody else might. A JuicyWoman understands that it is a basic need for every man and woman to feel special and desired by their partner. So she makes a point of dazzling her man, not only with her gorgeousness, but also by bestowing regular sexy comments and affectionate attention upon him.

＆ ❤ ❤ ❤ ＆

An enlightened woman is a woman who realises
that every second of the day
is only for feeding Love.

＆ ❤ ❤ ❤ ＆

65

Make Time to Fall in Love

You hear a woman say, *"I love my husband, but I'm not in love with him"*. And you can see it in her face that she wishes that was not the case. It is not uncommon for men to feel this way about their spouse either. Somehow these couples have neglected their relationship for so long that neither of them is enchanted by it any more. The practicalities of life have somehow drowned any excitement and thrill that might have existed when they first met.

In all intimate relationships, if you want to have the sweetest, most glorious and loving of relationships, you must have regular 'fall-in-love' times. What is a 'fall-in-love' time? It is the all-important period when you and your man spend time away together. Away from the house, away from work, away from the children, away from the mundane. Socialising with other couples doesn't count. It has to be when you both are devoting the occasion to each other as individuals. It could be a nice, romantic meal at a favourite restaurant. It could be going to the theatre and holding hands while you're being entertained. Or it could be a long, leisurely stroll on the beach. 'Fall-in-love' time can be as elaborate as a weekend stay in a foreign city or as simple as a picnic by the river. The essential ingredient is that you are both enjoying each other's company without being distracted by the phone (mobile phones are switched off at this point), work, children, TV or other people.

'Fall-in-love' time is vital if you want to have an exceptional relationship with your beloved. It is the lucrative investment that shifts your relationship from an ordinary to an *extraordinary* level. It is the rewarding outlay that transforms your relationship from a semi-precious one into a brilliant diamond. You need this regular time-out so that you can give your undivided attention to each other. After all, you eat, sleep and breathe with this man, so why shouldn't he become the dearest and most enchanting creature to you? And the only way he's going to be enchanting is when you can see him beyond the roles he plays. As long as you can only see the husband, the father, the breadwinner, you don't know your man. And vice versa. What are his hopes and dreams? What are his wildest aspirations in life? Does he know the same about you? Quality time together without any distraction allows you both to enquire more deeply into each other's heart. In the process of exploring the answers, you not only get to know him better, but you get to know yourself a lot better too. Life is then an ongoing, amazing journey of self-discovery rather than a relentless ride on a monotonous track.

We often care for our plants and animals better than we care for our intimate relationship. We take the time and effort to give them what they need in order to flourish, but we are too busy to do the same for the man we love. Just observe the amount of fuss and affection we lavish on our animals; our man will turn into Prince Charming if only we shower him with half that affection!

Having regular 'fall-in-love' time allows you to appreciate your other half for the man he truly is. And he too gets the chance to notice again how beautiful you look when you smile. His heart can be warmed again by the same feelings he felt for you when you first fell in love with each other; when you were generous and gave each other hours of your time. By spending this quality time together, it gives you both a chance to update in a personal and intimate way. Being away gives you the quiet, undistracted attention that allows you to notice sweet details about each other that are otherwise missed. You will be amazed how many delightful subtleties are being drowned out by the noisy ins and outs of your daily life.

You will know intimately what inspires him, what he cares deeply about. This 'fall-in-love' time gives you both a chance to appreciate each other on a regular basis. You only talk about yourself and each other. This keeps the fire of romance burning.

What are the consequences of not having these regular, all-important times? One, you take each other for granted. Two, romance is subtly murdered. Three, you will feel unappreciated for the woman you are, while he feels he is just the provider, the repairman and the babysitter for your nights out with the girls. You are partners, but you are not friends. You don't give your best to each other. Instead, you give your frustrations, your irritations and resentments to each other. You poison the relationship without realising that is what you are both doing. You also have unrealistic expectations of each other. You lose the friendship. And, over a long period of time, you may live in the same house, but you become estranged from each other. This leaves a gaping hole in your relationship, draining it of its vital life force and Love. This leaves your relationship vulnerable to outside forces. This is when affairs take place.

Whenever you have your couple time, consider it a date with each other. Just because you've been married for the last twenty or thirty years, it doesn't mean you should stop wooing each other. Make the effort to look good, for him but especially for yourself too. Wear something that makes you feel feminine and radiant. Or wear what he would like you to wear. Give your hair the polish it needs, be it a good cut or colour. Adorn your gorgeous self with some beautiful jewellery. This always makes you feel and look gorgeous because the sparkle and shine reminds you of your intrinsic radiance and light.

When you are out on a date with your man, let him take charge completely. Let him decide where to take you. Let him surprise you. Don't tell him where to park the car, even though you may have spotted the perfect place. Let him order your scrumptious meal for you. Don't do anything. Just sit back and mesmerise him with your gorgeousness and femininity. Allow him to *lead* you, while you *surrender* into his Love and adoration for you. In other words, let him be the man while you bask in the delicious joy of being an adored woman. This charming arrangement will make you shine and radiate brighter than the glorious full moon.

How often should you have this 'us time'? Once a month works wonders. Stretch it to six weeks if you have to. These emotional investments will give you generous returns in your relationship. It won't be long before you rediscover the man you fell madly in love with all those years ago. It will also make your mundane life more magnificent. Having given this precious time to each other, when you both enter into your normal everyday routine again, there will be an added glow and warmth to it. It is important for you to fix the date in advance; put it on the calendar. You can move it around if need be, but at least it's there for you both to see and look forward to. Having it in the diary shows the priority you are giving to this commitment to excel in the personal and intimate areas of your life. Your relationship will be a living entity for both of you again, where the man he is, and the woman you are, are deeply nourished by its sanctity and blessedness.

A JuicyWoman guards her relationship with her man jealously. As Love sits in her soul, her man sits at the altar of her heart. Her Love is her daily offering to him. And the time when it is dedicated to each other alone is their offering to their relationship. This ultimately results in a happier woman and a happier man. The happiness scales can once again creak under the weight of their increased Joy!

A woman who only uses her lips
to utter heart-soothing sounds
is a woman who understands that Love works.

66

The Art of Getting What You Want Without Nagging

To your man, when you repeat what you have already asked of him, it can come across as nagging. And nagging doesn't work because it brings out the rebel in him. When you nag, subconsciously he digs his heels in deeper. He switches to 'child mode' because when you nag, you do a 'mother' on him. The same old drone makes the man switch off. Watch his face glaze over as he tunes you out.

We are inherently different from our menfolk. We love talking because we bond through words, through the sounds of empathy we make with each other. We love talking because we build emotional connections through the process of verbal communication. Our menfolk, however, would much rather be in action than talk. This is because men are goal-driven while women are experience-oriented. So nagging our man to get what we want is futile, a total waste of time.

What we don't realise is that the moment we nag him, we shape-shift from being an attractive, feminine woman that he desires, to being his mother. A man is not turned on by a woman who tells him what to do. In fact, it's the quickest way to turn a man off, because when we nag him, he no longer feels a hero to us. And a man who is hero-worshipped by his woman is more helpful towards her because pleasing her makes him feel masculine. So, if you want to stay attractive to your man, don't nag. Okay, so you feel he takes you for granted. What can you do to get his attention? Communicate with action, not words. Pull back a little. Stay a little aloof. It will catch him by surprise and get his attention big time, especially if you are usually affectionate and open towards him. If you just nag, it reassures him that you are still there, waiting for him. He presses the mute button to cut out your monotonous sound and, as you wave your hands about like a demented octopus, it gives him a quiet assurance that you are still there giving him attention. It doesn't give him anything to be concerned about or ponder over. You keep pushing into him with your barrage of sounds so he doesn't need to come out and meet you. In fact, you could be so in his face that he would rather you back off and leave him alone. But when you pull back during those times, after a while he is likely to feel your energetic absence and wonder where you've gone. That will intrigue him and pull him in. Remember, for men, actions speak louder than words. It is with your behaviour, not your words, that you let him know where you stand.

Use the fact that men are territorial creatures. Tell him not to worry about those shelves that he promised to put up in the study six months ago. Tell him you know he is a busy guy, so you've asked Alan next door to put them up for you. Tell him Alan seems to relish the thought of rescuing a damsel in distress. If your man has any masculine pride, he will make sure those shelves are properly up before your neighbour gets the chance to be a hero in your eyes.

Another way of getting what you want without nagging your man is to treat him like you would treat a friend—with courtesy and respect. If you haven't got anything nice to say, don't say anything at all. Observe and see what your overall dynamic with your partner is. Do you generally put his back up by criticising him? If you want to get the best out of him, you have to ignore negative behaviour and praise the positive instead. You need to focus on what is right, rather than what is wrong. By changing the way you relate to him, you will find that he responds back in kind with more thoughtful actions and consideration for your feelings.

Let your man know what makes you happy, not what makes you angry. A man who loves his woman will want to please her whenever he can. Reward him with huge smiles and delicious hugs when he gets it right. Magnify your pleasure by jumping up and down, as if you can hardly contain your happiness. Believe me, he lives for those moments.

A JuicyWoman keeps her integrity intact by not going down the nagging route. She can see clearly that a woman stands a better chance of getting her own way by staying attractive, while nagging actually 'uglifies' her. She also knows that when it comes to verbally communicating with her man, less is more. When her man falls asleep in the relationship and takes her for granted, she uses her body language to communicate her feelings. The more feminine and inviting she is, the quicker he wakes up. And when she pulls away because he hasn't been playing ball, he will soon gravitate towards her again with his full attention. Body talk is infinitely more effective when it comes to the opposite sex.

Juicy Sisterhood

❧ ❤ ❤ ❤ ❧

A woman who nurtures every woman she meets
with her presence
drinks from the fountain of golden life.

❧ ❤ ❤ ❤ ❧

67

Looking at Women Through New Eyes

One of our biggest resources for strength, support, power and inspiration is our fellow women. Because we are from the same pool and our hormones share the same matrix, it is much easier for women to relate to each other and to be each other's greatest support. There is a quiet understanding between all women because we feel the same in our female bones. Our resilience is second to none as we endure whatever challenges life throws at us and still we rise stronger and more beautiful than ever. Our tenacity to live and protect our young ones in times of hardship goes far beyond the most punishing task the human heart can endure. We have double the X factor in our chromosomes (XY for men but XX for women!) so in truth we are more amazing than we realise.

Only a tiny fraction of our intuitive wisdom has thus far been accessed. Our ability to love reaches beyond the far ends of our galaxy. It is said that the closest resemblance of divine Love in the physical dimension is the love a mother feels for her child. Therefore, if we so choose, women can be our greatest ally. There is a huge reservoir of untapped intuitive power and feminine resource in women. The more we understand and embrace this truth, the quicker we heal ourselves and the world. Once we've healed, we can bring heaven to earth.

To access this vast feminine resource, we must look at our fellow women through new eyes. Start to see women with benevolence. See the good in every woman, no matter how obscure this good may seem to us, and no matter how irate we may feel in the moment about their behaviour. The more we practise this kindness and compassion, the more peace we will feel in our own heart. Should you perceive a woman acting unkindly towards you, practise looking beyond the appearance of her actions. Question your heart to see if there is anything you need to correct or align within yourself. Perhaps she is only a messenger, sent to help you liberate an inner blockage that stands in the way of your joy? Or maybe she is here to teach you to be more generous-hearted towards those who challenge your patience. Everything has its gift for us when we open our mind and humble our heart to receive it. Knowing that, we can endeavour to practise loving the souls of those who push our buttons, even if we may not warm to their personality.

We need to see that we are part of this wondrous collective entity called Woman. We need each other's support through the ebb and flow of life. You can uplift me when it's my turn to feel down. I can inspire you when you've momentarily forgotten your own wisdom. What you and I can do for each other through the seasons of our lives can make our lives infinitely sweeter and more beautiful. Only a woman's heart can understand the depth of another woman's sorrow. Only a woman's spirit can understand why a woman feels the way she does. It takes a woman to truly know another woman. As women, we never stand alone. When one hurts, we all hurt. When one wins, we all win. When we apply this law of oneness, the power and effectiveness we yield is immense. The quicker we start living as a collective, the better the quality of our own life will be. The sooner we start treating everyone as if they are our own, the more wondrous our life will be.

A JuicyWoman knows she is part of the collective whole; every other woman lives in her and she lives in each of them. Fat, thin, ugly or beautiful, she is all of them. Every woman is a friend in disguise. Because there is no separation in her heart, she has direct access to the unlimited power of the feminine.

There is a secret place
where every woman is deeply nourished
divinely inspired
and lovingly held in feminine arms
- Sisterhood

68

How We Limit This Vast Feminine Power

Although we are part of this vast resource of feminine strength and beauty, not many women are able to access it due to their own non-integral behaviour. Each time we behave in a way that violates this sacred 'sister-heart', we cut ourselves off from its nourishing source. We lose the biggest collaborator in goodness, the dearest friend when we are in need. How do we defile this holy covenant? How do we let the collective Woman and our own feminine self down?

- By speaking ill of other women or ourselves
- By criticising other women or ourselves
- By gossiping about other women's behaviour
- By being jealous or envious of other women's glory
- By dating a married man
- By stealing another woman's man
- By marrying for money rather than Love
- By fleecing a man through divorce
- By prostituting your integrity for outer gains
- By doubting your own excellence

We must learn to undo our non-integral habits if we are to reach the summit of our happiness. When we speak ill of other women or ourselves, we are tearing holes in our own garment of womanhood. Gossiping about another woman's behaviour is simply a cover-up for our own inadequacies and low self-opinion. We need to realise that if we think nothing of stealing another woman's man, then we must be prepared to have the same happen to us when we're blissfully happy in our relationship. As for fleecing a man through divorce because we legally can, we are exchanging our nobility for cash. The money may clothe our shameless body and feed our greedy stomach, but our feminine soul will slowly shrivel up and die an undignified death. Only Love can be our raiment. And only Love is our nourishment.

Only when we refuse to compromise our radiance for temporal rewards will our strength and creative power return. Then, 24/7 access to this incredible pool of feminine support and soul sustenance will be available to us in our hour of need. We will never feel isolated or forgotten again. Our sisters will make sure we are always held in Love, no matter what. Men will honour us as noble women again because we respect and honour ourselves and refuse to trade our integrity for anything. They will stop being aggressive towards us and treat us with kindness and tenderness because we won't have a chip on our shoulder about being a woman, believing that we have to fight men in order to excel in the world. They will also trust us with their heart again because they are no longer worried that we will rob them of their hard-earned cash. The more we walk with dignity, decency and grace, the more radiant and beautiful we become. The more each of us embodies the Love we are, the more fulfilled and happy women will be on this planet.

Don't feel guilty if you have been one to criticise or gossip about other women. Or if you have dated married men, or even ended up living with one. We cannot change the past. So don't beat yourself up and think that things won't improve for you. We have all been there, and done things we are not proud of, not because we're nasty women, but because we were afraid. Afraid of not being good enough or afraid of not getting what we wanted. Now that we are aware what we have been doing to ourselves, we can apply this awareness and start afresh. What matters is NOW. The power to reshape your life is in the now; not yesterday, and not tomorrow either. Forgive and be at peace. Then move forward with the resolve to walk tall, with integrity. Be your majestic self. Be the woman you're proud to be. Be the Love you already are.

A JuicyWoman will do her best not to desecrate the purity and breathtaking beauty of womanhood by making fear-induced decisions. There is no need for her to steal another woman's man, as she is totally capable of attracting her own. Instead of being jealous about another woman's glory, she allows it to inspire her. She is always nourished by another woman's joy. This makes her own joy totally accessible and abundant.

You are meant to walk on this earth
in your full radiance.

You are meant to bless life
with your feminine gifts.

You are meant to live happily ever after
as who you are.

Don't delay this miracle for a moment longer.

69

Staying Juicy Indefinitely

We are living in incredibly exciting times in terms of human consciousness. Many changes are taking place as we become more aware of the power of thought, and the direct role we play in shaping our lives. We are also seeing the significance of co-operating and working together for the good of humanity. Together, the load becomes much lighter and the experience of day-to-day living becomes sweeter. In fact, the juicier you are, the sweeter your life will be. We need to take the appropriate steps to nurture our gorgeous juiciness. Is there a way to stay Juicy forever? Regardless of how the seasons age us, is it still possible to ooze juiciness and dazzle the world with our radiance? The answer to this Juicy question is Yes! Yes! Yes! Just because the body ages (the less fear, the slower the ageing process), we don't have to become rigid and unyielding or dress ourselves in grey. Our most powerful aspect is our Juicy spirit, a spiritual rainbow-light that illuminates every substance it passes through. It is the death-defying, nothing-is-impossible spiritual self that knows that Love can never die. We were this Love before our human birth, and we shall remain as this Love when the body crumbles away. Whatever our human personality goes through, this part of us remains untouched and untainted. Harnessing this spiritual force within us is the key to staying Juicy indefinitely.

Be happy. Stay grateful. Every day, take a moment to notice how blessed you are. The mere fact you're alive and breathing is a tremendous blessing to begin with. Birds sing for your innate joy and flowers bloom to remind you of your intrinsic beauty. Find all the things that are right in your life and appreciate each one wholeheartedly. Ignore the rest. The law of attraction says that what you focus your attention on, you will get more of. Take joy and delight in the simplest of things. Maintain a generous attitude towards everything and everyone that crosses your path. Through this generosity, you will experience your own boundless nature, abundant beyond any limitation your mind can conjure up when it is in fear.

You are what you eat, so make a point of eating with *quality* in mind, rather than *quantity*. Make sure you drink enough water. We wouldn't dream of not flushing the toilet after using it, so why wouldn't we make sure our internal system is regularly cleansed throughout the day? Keep your body supple and healthy through yoga, tai chi or similar workouts. Yoga and tai chi are among the few physical disciplines that exercise and regenerate your internal organs. 'Use it' so you won't have to 'lose it'. Make time to dance, not only in a formal setting but also whenever you feel like it, on your own or with your female companions. Let your body whirl and twirl with delight, until you become poetry in motion. You will start to love being vibrantly alive.

Let your mind be open, at all times. Life is abundantly full of gifts and blessings, and we receive so much when we're open. Practise meditation. Join a group or find a good teacher to learn this powerful technique. One by one, every fearful thought can be weeded out, leaving you unhindered and free to be the glorious woman you are meant to be. Through meditation and inner work, you will also come to know your deepest gift, and your heart will sing when you can offer this gift of who you are to life in every moment. Get in touch with your wild streak, that undomesticated self that is passionately creative and bold. Every woman is creative, so don't let the voice from childhood say, *"I can't sing"*, *"I'm lousy at dancing"* or *"I can't draw to save my life."* If you can talk, you can sing. If you can walk, you can dance. If you can hold a pen, you can draw. Don't compare what you can do with what others can do, period. To compare yourself with anyone, especially people who have done hours of training, is to murder your own talent before it gets the chance to be born.

Join a group and study together to enhance your spiritual development. Your true power lies in your spiritual self, so give this part of you top priority in your everyday life. There are thousands of good books out there. Read something worthwhile every day. Check out good courses or seminars to attend so you can keep expanding your awareness and develop your spiritual understanding. Knowledge is power. The power to reshape your life and to be a blessing is yours when you put in the effort.

As well as having great women, past or present, to inspire you, commit to being a role model for your daughters, friends and people around you. Be the person you want to be. Be the person you feel happy and at peace with. Treat yourself with love and gentleness. Treat others the same. Remember that gentleness is one of the keys to our feminine strength and power.

Support all women, and together we can make sisterhood into a universal force for healing, for peace, for total bliss of the heart. Have good woman friends, ones that inspire and motivate you to unlock more of your potential. Meet up regularly and nourish each other with your love and friendship. Only the company of good women can nourish your feminine soul. Don't be afraid to speak the truth with each other, no matter how difficult you may think it is for the other person to hear. A good friend is willing to put her friendship on the line because she wants to serve her friend more than she needs to be liked by her. Make a point of celebrating and sharing joy with each other when one of you has done well. Get together, have a pleasant meal and toast her success. There is no need for us to feel envious or jealous of another woman's accomplishment. Jealousy or envy only dulls your own radiance; celebrating her success paves the way for your own success.

Be part of a community or group that offers help and support to all those who are in need, especially women. The more we help our sisters, the more our communities will thrive, because we are central to life around us. A happy woman automatically means a happy wife, mother, sister, daughter and friend.

A JuicyWoman knows that juiciness can only be drawn from the deep well of her spiritual self. Until the last breath escapes her lips, she never takes her attention away from her spiritual growth and awareness. She knows that if she doesn't live the glorious truth of who she truly is, no one else will. And if she doesn't offer her unique gifts to life, no one else can.

You are not who you think you are.
You are more amazing than you believe.
You are Love itself. And so is everything and everyone else.
Know this fundamental truth and begin to live as Love.
The whole play of life is simply Love giving itself to itself,
in every moment, in every place.
Herein lies the end of separation.
And herein lies the bliss that you have been waiting for.

- Ocean WhiteHawk
9th May 2009.

Visit www.oceanwhitehawk.com and redesign your life for inner bliss.

- Learn more about courses, seminars and one-on-one work with Ocean WhiteHawk.

- Find out more about the life-changing Power to Reshape one-on-one course that overhauls the way you think, enhances your relationship with yourself and others and not only reshapes your outlook, but also your life.

- To book Ocean WhiteHawk for speaking events.

- To register for 365 JuicyWoman inspirational sayings to be sent to your mobile phone daily.

- For more information on JuicyWoman online study group.

- For Ocean WhiteHawk's books, CDs and DVDs.

- For more information about ConfidentWoman – a charitable organisation founded by Ocean WhiteHawk which offers free courses and coaching to help and support women with limited financial means, to develop a healthy self-esteem and vibrant confidence in their personal and working life.